LIES
SALON
OWNERS
BELIEVE

and

THE TRUTH THAT
SETS THEM FREE

LIES
SALON
OWNERS
BELIEVE

and

THE TRUTH THAT
SETS THEM FREE

Dan Lok
DJ Richoux

Advantage®

Published by Advantage, Charleston, South Carolina.
Member of Advantage Media Group.
ADVANTAGE is a registered trademark and the Advantage colophon is a trademark of Advantage Media Group, Inc.

Printed in the United States of America.
ISBN: 978-159932-270-4
LCCN: 2011905667

Advantage Media Group is proud to be a part of the Tree Neutral® program. Tree Neutral offsets the number of trees consumed in the production and printing of this book by taking proactive steps such as planting trees in direct proportion to the number of trees used to print books. To learn more about Tree Neutral, please visit **www.treeneutral.com**. To learn more about Advantage's commitment to being a responsible steward of the environment, please visit **www.advantagefamily.com/green**

Advantage Media Group is a leading publisher of business, motivation, and self-help authors. Do you have a manuscript or book idea that you would like to have considered for publication? Please visit **www.amgbook.com** or call **1.866.775.1696**

DEDICATION

We dedicate this book to all the salon and spa owners

that still have a dream of having more freedom,

more profits and more fun in their business.

FOREWORD

by Jay Conrad Levinson

I read a lot of business books. I also write a lot of them, 58 authored or coauthored at this point. My books have sold more than 21 million copies in 62 languages. But when I read *Lies Salon Owners Believe*, I felt like a little kid. Here I was, a 77-year old author and speaker, yet wide-eyed and tingling with excitement at the words and wisdom of Dan Lok and DJ Richoux in this brilliant book.

In these pages, Dan and DJ have taught me a lot of crucial things that I never knew. I felt as innocent as that little kid.

They take a seemingly complex topic and simplify it to the point that any salon owner who reads these pages and doesn't go on to lead a stress-free and wealth-abundant life really ought to question his or her existence.

They mark a clear path to success, then illuminate it with so many examples, specifics, and just plain darned good writing that you'll start wondering why salon owners aren't lined up for miles to own and read this book.

Luckily for you, they aren't. But once the word gets out about the extraordinary insights in this book, you'll find that the competition is a whole lot keener.

In this book, Dan starts out as a rank beginner, which in the world of salons, he certainly was. He takes readers by the hand and leads them through the minefields of reality to the hallowed ground of timeless knowledge that they can use for the rest of their lives.

Because of the utter simplicity of the authors' writing and thinking, you'll find that it's a cinch to act upon everything you'll learn. And that's exactly what you must do. Dan and DJ do all the thinking for you. All that's left for you is the doing. And that's actually going to be fun.

Just as this book started out intriguingly and then got better, you'll discover that running a successful salon will be the same way.

When you do the work – yes, there is work involved – and do it with the proven system Dan uses, you'll discover that it gets easier and more enjoyable.

The myths and lies so commonly believed by salon owners are dissected in this book. Dan and DJ's insights bring you a fresh perspective and show you the reality and the truths to being successful in the salon business.

Not only will you look forward to going to work, you'll also look forward to applying all that you'll learn from the pages in this book. You'll look forward to achieving your goals and you'll look forward to spending your hard-earned – but not that hard-earned – money.

This book is warmed by the humanity that Dan has brought into each chapter. It is nourished by the sustenance he has included in the mind-set of a successful salon owner. This will soon be your mind-set, your ticket to ride first class into your new life as a flourishing businessman or business woman. Make no mistake. Being a successful salon owner requires that you also become a successful business owner. There are differences, you know.

This book spells out the differences and shows you how to be as good at business as you are at making people look and feel exquisite.

You're going to love your transformation.

Jay Conrad Levinson,
The Father of Guerrilla Marketing
Author, "Guerrilla Marketing" series of books, DeBary, Florida

DAN AND DJ'S MISSION

Dan and DJ want to empower women to become role models to their children like their own mothers have been a role model to them. Dan's parents got divorced when he was 16 years old. He was raised by his mother. She's always been supportive of Dan and believed in Dan despite all of his crazy business ventures including his crazy teenage antics like wanting to quit school. Through all his ups and downs, she has always believed in Dan.

One of the reasons they want to empower women around the world is for the simple reason that studies and anecdotal evidence shows that most significant changes and impact will come from girls and women.

Greg Mortenson, Founder of the Central Asia Institute and author of the best- selling book "Three Cups of Tea" said the following...

"Once you educate the boys, they tend to leave the villages and go search for work in the cities," Moternson explains. "But the girls stay home, become leaders in the community, and pass on what they've learned. If you really want to change a culture, to empower women, improve basic hygiene and health care, and fight high rates of infant mortality, the answer is to educate the girls

WHY KIVA?

Kiva works and is empowering women entrepreneurs every day! Kiva makes loans that change lives.

Dan and DJ believe that former president; Bill Clinton said it best...

"If you look at Kiva.org, people with a **very modest amount of money can make a huge positive impact all around the world**. There are so many people who want to give but don't really know how to do it. Through Kiva.org, people around the world can become micro-bankers to developing world entrepreneurs, who have their own ideas, so we can give them a chance to raise their kids with dignity, send their kids to school, and in troubled places like Afghanistan we can marginally increase the chance that peace can prevail, because people will see there is a positive alternative to conflict."

WHY DAN AND DJ SUPPORT KIVA?

As entrepreneurs and business owners, Dan and DJ love Kiva's model. Instead of costly offices, Kiva uses the internet to display micro entrepreneurs seeking a loan. As a lender, you can scroll through hundreds of businesses seeking a loan and select one that connects and resonates with you. You actually connect with the person seeking the loan as you can see their face, learn a little about their situation and discover the purpose of their loan. Thanks to a lean administration team and lender donations, Kiva passes on 100% of whatever you lend and you get the satisfaction of knowing who your money is helping.

Everyone needs a helping hand to reach their dreams. Dan and DJ recognize that they had a lot of help along the way. They have a soft spot for people less fortunate that are struggling in a tough physical and economic environment. All they need is a chance and a helping hand.

These people don't want a hand out; they want an opportunity to make a better life for themselves and their family. They want to have a chance to live a life of dignity.

Dan can relate as he came to Canada to make a better life for himself and his mother. He was born in Hong Kong and when he came to Canada many years ago he had no money, no connections, and not a word of the English language on his lips. English was NOT his first language. **All he wanted was an opportunity.**

100% of the author's profits from the sale of this book will be used to support Kiva.

HOW YOU CAN HELP

At Salon Business Expert, we are building a Kiva community (lending team) of salon and spa owners that are devoted to empowering beauty business owners around the world.

The mission of the community is to help other less fortunate struggling salon owners that are in tough physical and economic environments build a better future for themselves and their families.

PAY IT FORWARD, HELP GROW OUR COMMUNITY

As your dreams and goals of having More Freedom, More Profits and More Fun begin to come true for you, I ask you to be the spark that starts another women entrepreneurs dream. Consider helping a micro entrepreneur in less than ideal conditions and circumstances enter the world of entrepreneurship by joining the Salon Business Expert Community Lending Team. Kiva enables you to lend small amounts of money (loans start at $25) to entrepreneurs in the developing world.

For more information and to join the team go to:

www.salonbusinessexpert.com/kiva.html

TABLE OF CONTENTS

Introduction   **19**

How I Raise Myself from Failure to Success   23
Now Meet DJ Richoux, The Book's CoAuthor   26
What Makes This Book Different   28
What's Holding You Back?   29

**Lie #1 – "I Just Need To Be Good At What I Do,
And My Business Will Be Successful."**   **33**

You Are Not Alone!   36
Being the Best Salon Is Not Good Enough   37
It's NOT Your Fault   37
How I Accidentally Became A Salon Owner   38
The Biggest Reason Why Salon Owners Fail   44
How To Make All Your Dreams A Reality   48
How I Discovered My New Life Direction   51
Are You Working So Hard, But Still Aren't Getting What You Want From
Your Salon /Spa Business?   55

**Lie #2 – The Salon Business Can Only Be A Good "Hobby Business"
Or A "Labor Of Love."**   **59**

Why Anyone - Including You - Can Be Wealthy   63
Do You Own A Job Instead Of A Business   65
Are You Guilty Of Committing This Deadly Sin?   66
The Most Common Mistakes Struggling Salon Owners Make   67
Why You Deserve To Be Fulfilled And Wealthy At The Same Time   70
The Only Reason To Be In Any Business   70
Become Financially Free And Live Your Dreams   71

**Lie #3 – "It's A Business, It's Supposed To Be Hard Work
And Long Hours – It'll Get Better."**   **75**

A Valuable Lesson I Learned About Building Businesses   78
Why Most Salon Businesses Are Hard Work - If they Don't Miserably Fail   78
Are You Trapped In Your Business?   81
What To Do If You Want To Turn Your Salon/Spa Business Around Immediately   81
No Decent Beauty or Hair Professional Would Say That Being "Self Taught" Is a Good Idea   83
Work ON Your Business – Not Just IN Your Business   84
Why Repetitive, Time-Consuming Tasks Might Be Your Downfall   86
My Super-Simple Productivity Secret   88

Lie #4 – "We Just Need To Get Our Name Out There."   **93**

What Advertising Sales Reps Don't Want You To Know   94
An Easy Way To Adopt The Mindset Of Successful And Wealthy Salon Owners   97
How To Double Or Triple Your Salon Profits   98
Brand-Image Advertising VS. Promotional Advertising   99

Four Important Rules Of Promotional Advertising 102
What Real Marketing Is Not 103
What Real Marketing Really Is 104
Look Over Dan's Shoulder 106
A New Way Of Getting Clients That Really Works 108
The Quickest, Easiest And Best Way To Get A Never-Ending Supply Of Clients 110
Feeling Frustrated and Overwhelmed? Need My Help? 111

Lie #5 - "If Only I Could Get More Clients In The Door, My Business Will Be Successful…" **115**

The Single Most Important Asset in Your Business 117
Uncover the Hidden Profits in Your Business Today 118
How to Keep Your Current Clients Coming Back Again and Again 119
The Two Essential Ingredients of a Thriving Salon Business 121
Six Powerful Reasons Why You Should Launch a Loyalty Program 126
Plug the Hole in the Bottom of Your Income Bucket 128
More Profit – More Time Off – Fewer Hassles 130

Lie #6 – "I Have To Lower My Prices To Beat Out My Competition." **135**

The Most Important Lesson I Have Learned About Pricing 139
How to Go From the Bottom of the Ladder Straight to the Top 140
We Can Make It Up In Volume 142
How I Position My Salon to Charge Above -Average Prices 143
Eliminate and Repel Bargain Pricing Customers 144
What Really Matters to Your Clients 146
You are NOT Your Client 147
High Prices = Better Clients 148
How to Identify Your Ideal Client 149
Creating the Right Experience for Your Clients 151
There are MORE Reasons to Go Higher! 153
Low is Not the Way to Go 156

Lie #7 – "I Could Do This On My Own" **161**

The Unvarnished Truth About What It Really Takes to Succeed 167
Four Exit Strategies for Your Salon Business 168
I Became a Better Leader When I Learned This 169
Set a High Standard for Your Salon 170
Establish a Working System for Your Salon 172
Getting Your Staff to Support Your New System 173
The Most Important Person to Make All Your Dreams a Reality 174
How I Found My Mentors (and How You Can, Too) 176
The Shortcut to Creating the Salon Business You've Always Imagined (but Still Have a Life) 178
How Do You Find The Right Mentor for You? 181

CONCLUSION **183**

INTRODUCTION

Imagine this.

It's sometime between 9 a.m. and 10 a.m. You drive up to the parking lot of your salon, and immediately notice the assigned parking spots for your salon are taken up.

That's definitely a good thing. It automatically means happy clients are already inside the salon and a busy profitable day lies ahead.

You walk up to your salon and see your large, illuminated, professional-looking salon sign. It sends chills down your spine as you think, "Very classy."

Your salon windows are sparkling clean – so clean you can clearly see your own reflection in the glass.

As you walk in, you can see all the stations are full and your salon is packed with clients.

You say "Hi" to your salon manager or coordinator and she tells you the good news.

The salon is fully booked for the day. Still, she's received a few calls this morning from clients wanting to be squeezed in.

But they will have to be squeezed in next week. Your staff is already over-booked for this week.

Your salon manager or coordinator, who is very competent, runs the day-to-day operations with ease. She's typically busy helping your staff with small tasks, or on the phone answering inquiries and booking appointments. Her excellent customer service skills keep your clients happy! You can count on her to handle any situation – big or small.

Your clients love your salon services. Price is not an issue for them, because they see incredible value in the services you are providing.

They don't just book a single service. They frequently book multiple services at the same time – it saves them time, and ensures them an appointment spot.

In addition, your clients are happy and loyal. They keep coming back again and again and refer their family and friends.

Your cash register is consistently busy as your manager rings in sales transaction after transaction.

Ka-ching!

It's a wonderful feeling to have – knowing there's money in the bank.

With a steady flow of cash coming into your bank account, you're not financially stressed or cash-strapped.

Your monthly expenses are paid on time.

You easily plan and budget for salon upgrades or large product purchases.

You may come in for just three or four days a week.

By spending less time in your salon business, you have the time and freedom to enjoy doing the things you've always wanted to do and love!

Imagine going on a vacation, staying in a luxury resort in an exotic place like Italy, Rome, Paris, Mexico, the Bahamas, or the Cayman Islands. You could be there by yourself, with a loved one, with your family, experiencing a whole new exciting culture, a lifestyle native to the region, mixing with the locals or just relaxing having a great time!

You relax in the spa. Soak up the sun lying in the pool or lying on a lounge chair.

You take evening walks with your loved ones on the beach. You enjoy watching the sun setting and feeling the sand in your toes.

Your meals are taken care of – no cooking required, just eat out whatever you want whenever you want for your entire vacation.

You don't have to tidy up your bedroom – that's what housekeeping is for.

You can take the day off from your kids if you want. Hotel resorts are known for their kids clubs where children are entertained from daytime through to the evening.

Or you can stay close to home and…

> … take up scrapbooking! (Create lasting memories of yourself and family, big events like weddings, graduations, birthdays. You can even preserve sentimental value of those can't-bear-to-throw-away things like concert tickets, friendship bracelets from your childhood years, etc.)

> … throw a jewelry party! (Invite your friends over and have a blast trying on bracelets, necklaces, earrings, and all the bling you can get your hands on!)

> … host a cooking party! (Imagine the quick and easy appetizers you can make with any ingredient!)

> … learn how to make soap – from scratch! (It makes great gifts!)

> … learn to dance with your partner! (Pick up a couple of new moves with salsa dancing, ballroom dancing or even belly dancing!)

> … learn a new language like Spanish? (Can you say "Buenos dias"?)

… take up a creative writing course? (Get those creative juices flowing! Learn how to write short stories, novels, and even poems!)

Or just spend quality time with your family, friends, and loved ones, doing simple things like:

… going for long lunches (one-on-one)

… going shopping (checking out new arrivals in clothes, electronics etc.)

… watching movies (maybe even back-to-back movies!)

… enjoying the day at the golf course (what's your handicap?)

… going for a family paintball adventure (sounds like lots of fun!)

… taking the kids to karate lessons, sporting activities, ballet classes (watching them make progress in their skills).

All this is possible when you have a well-managed salon business that's successful and profitable!

You are not trapped in your business – rather, you have control over your own life.

You can comfortably live in a home that you own.

You can drive the car you've always wanted.

You can give your children a fun and enjoyable life, filled with adventures/activities and memories.

Your salon business can truly support your family and your lifestyle.

HOW I RAISED MYSELF FROM FAILURE TO SUCCESS

My name is Dan Lok. I was born in Hong Kong.

I came to Vancouver, Canada, in 1995 with no money, no connections, and not a word of the English language on my lips. English was NOT my first language.

Even today, I still speak with an accent! Some of my friends even tell me I still speak like Jackie Chan!

I knew I had to take care of my family and myself because my mom and dad got divorced when I was very young. I have always wanted to make something out of myself and provide a better lifestyle for my family.

When I was in high school, I started my first business with my friend, mowing lawns for people in our neighbourhood. The lawn-mowing business went extremely well, except we didn't have customers!

On and off, I would start a business and it would fail very quickly. I was working very hard but I was never making any money. I'll never forget the conversation I had with my mom when I came home one evening just totally depressed and exhausted.

"Dan, you're killing yourself," my mom said. "I know you love me, but we don't have to be wealthy. You don't have to make a lot of money. You don't have to work this hard."

"I know, Mom," I said. "But if I don't make a lot of money, I will never be able to buy you a home."

"Dan. It's OK. You don't have to buy me a home. I am fine," said my mom.

I insisted, "Mom, I know I don't I have to, but I want to. It's the least I could do for you."

The lowest point of my life was when I got a job in a local super-market, making minimum wage as a grocery bagger. (That was the only job I've ever been hired for. I've never worked for anyone else but myself since then.)

I was dead broke. Life was a struggle. Making ends meet was tough. I was in debt and had trouble paying my bills.

The only asset I had was a "lemon" of a white Ford Escort with almost 150,000 miles on it. Yet, I was thankful for it because it got me from point A to point B. It was a means of transportation (barely) and I was able to get around.

I remember a local bakery that my mom and I used to drive to. We knew the bakery closed at 7 p.m. So we would wait until 6 p.m. and get there just in time as the bakery slashed the prices on all the bread it made for the day. We would end up getting five or six loaves of bread for just a couple bucks. We made that bread go a long way, as we ate it for breakfast and lunch every day for the entire week.

There was also a time in my life when my father suffered a stroke. He lives in Hong Kong. Unfortunately, I was so broke I couldn't even afford to purchase a plane ticket to go to Hong Kong to see him.

Life was indeed tough on me and my family.

But please, don't cry for me, because my life is not like that anymore.

Today, I enjoy a very comfortable lifestyle that I could not have imagined. I live in a beautiful place (a penthouse suite) with a great a view of the water. My mom and I no longer have to go to the bakery for discounted bread. Instead, I take my mom out to fancy restaurants including four- and five-star restaurants, as Vancouver is famous for its international cuisine.

Today, I no longer drive the "lemon" my white Ford Escort. I've upgraded to an exotic sports car, a Daytona Grey Audi R8 that I take out on sunny days. I also got a luxury SUV for Jennie, a black Audi

Q5. I own several businesses that have allowed me to lead this very comfortable lifestyle.

One of the businesses I own is a beauty salon in Vancouver called Sweet Nail.

When I started Sweet Nail, it was under the most undesirable circumstances. It was during the recession when people lost their jobs. Our local sales tax jumped from a manageable 5% to a whopping fat 12%. (Blame the government for this one!) And the salon was located in an area that is flooded with dozens of competitors.

Yet, I was able to make a healthy profit in my second month of business! I even had a waiting list of clients before Sweet Nail opened its doors!

In our first year in business, Sweet Nail generated more than $370,000 in gross sales and made a net profit of $120,000. This year, we have generated more than $200,000 in profits. Feel free to check out my salon website at www.sweetnailsalon.com. The phone number and address are listed on the site as well.

My salon business runs like clockwork, even when I am not there.

I mostly manage my salon at my own pace from my home office. And I spend only about four hours a week in my salon.

I am a happy salon owner, with nine very happy staff members who would never even think about leaving me. Often, our appointment book is filled up two weeks in advance.

I basically take time off whenever I want. Most of my time is spent ballroom dancing, practicing martial arts, reading books, writing, lunching with friends, traveling with my fiancé, and doing all the other fun stuff I love to do!

And yes, I have also taken my mom on a few holidays to show her my appreciation for all she's done.

Why am I sharing these things with you about my personal and business life?

It's not to impress you, but to inspire you and explain how good the salon business can be if you know some key pieces of information.

Remember, I opened my beauty salon in the middle of a recession and I was still able to turn in a profit in my second month!

I have this proven track record with Sweet Nail because I've spent more than a decade mastering the art of creating and running successful profitable businesses. And I've coached other business owners to do the same.

I think it's important if you're considering using me as a business mentor that you know my qualifications to see if I really can help you get results.

NOW MEET DJ RICHOUX, THE BOOK'S CO-AUTHOR

I met DJ Richoux in 2001 just when I was getting started in business. I had heard he was good at marketing and I needed some help as I was trying to build my little business. At first he would give me little assignments to do. I would go do the assignments, send him my results and then he would give me another assignment. After a couple of months he started giving me advice and suggestions as I tried to build my little business. Some of that advice was invaluable, as he saved me at least three years of hard work and struggle.

DJ is my go-to marketing expert. I have always relied on him for marketing advice because of his expertise. I keep in touch with him on a regular basis so I can bounce ideas and thoughts off him. He always gives me a fresh perspective and seems to have an insight or asks questions about something I never considered. Sometimes those questions have me going back to the drawing board reconsidering my plans.

Over the years I've grown, learned more, and made more mistakes. We've worked on various projects together. Whenever I have marketing challenges, I always pick up the phone to call DJ. He is on my speed dial.

I've always been the big-picture, idea, concept guy. A big thinker, action-oriented. DJ is the opposite, which is why I love to work with him. He's more grounded, more detail-oriented, more logical and systematic. That is what makes us a very powerful DUO.

Naturally, when I came up with the big idea of writing a book for salon owners, one of the first people I spoke to was DJ.

One afternoon over lunch, I approached DJ about my book idea.

"DJ, I'm seriously thinking about writing a book about the beauty industry," I said. "I really want to share with others how I started Sweet Nail and my experiences. I think it's important for salon owners out there to know there is hope, that the salon business can be a good business. They just need to be shown how to run a salon business that is fun to run and also profitable so they can also have some freedom. I want to get my message out there."

I continued, "There's an important section on marketing in the book. I think I've covered most areas. But if you would give me some feedback, it would be awesome. After all, several of the marketing concepts I'm referring to were originally introduced by you."

So DJ agreed to review the chapters on marketing. A couple of days later I heard back from him. Not only did he think the chapters on marketing were good, but he thought the rest of the book had a message every salon owner needed to hear. He gave me some suggestions and changes for most of the chapters.

Over the next month or so, we collaborated even more, fine-tuning each section of the book into a complete manuscript – ready for publishing.

That's when I suggested to him, "DJ, what do you think about being my coauthor? We've already worked together on a good portion of the book. And you have invested a considerable amount of your time and energy. Coauthoring seems to be the next natural step."

"Coauthor?" replied DJ. I sensed his hesitation. DJ didn't like working in the limelight, preferring to work in the operations side of things. Remember, he is a detail-oriented systems guy. "I have too much going on in my life now. Clients... other projects... I'll have to pass on this, Dan."

"Pass on it?" I exclaimed in disbelief. "DJ, you've helped me make this book 10 times better than it originally was. I would be honored if you would be my coauthor. Consider it my way of thanking you for your efforts and contribution. It's the MOST important book I've ever written. Your feedback is invaluable. You know me, I don't take no for an answer."

After I tried to persuade DJ a little more, he reluctantly agreed to be the coauthor of the book. What makes this book more valuable is you get my big-picture idea and concepts combined with DJ's more logical, systematic approach.

WHAT MAKES THIS BOOK DIFFERENT

I'm really excited to be sharing this information with you.

What you are about to learn has not only transformed my own life, but will literally change the lives of thousands and thousands of salon owners around the world.

I know that if you follow the strategies and secrets in this book, not only will you make more money, you will also have more freedom and have more fun than you ever dreamed possible. Stress and uncertainty will be things of the past.

This is NOT a typical book.

Rather, it's designed around the seven lies that are holding salon owners back. These lies can trip you up. They can keep you from expanding, from growing, from really enjoying your business, and from building a salon that supports your life instead of being a prisoner and slave to your business.

Being a salon owner myself, I've had to deal with these lies very quickly in order to be successful.

Each lie is designed to be a catalyst – something that will spark your own insights about your business, your finances, and yourself.

As each lie is addressed, I introduce my "Lokisms," which will open your eyes to a new world of understanding.

Think of them as "major lessons" and "understandings," in the sense that once you understand them, you'll never relate to your salon business, challenges or goals in the same way again.

Also, to make the book easier to read, I use generic terms like salon, staff or employees. When I use the words salon or day spa, it means your business, regardless of whether it is a hair salon, beauty salon, nail salon, tanning salon, pet spa, or day spa.

When I use the words staff or employees, it means your people, your team.

They could be the lead stylists, receptionists, salon assistants, salon coordinators, salon managers, spa managers, creative directors, nail technicians, hair stylists, color specialists, makeup artists, laser technicians, estheticians, or massage therapists, etc.

WHAT'S HOLDING YOU BACK?

As you go through this book, there may be mental obstacles that come up. You might start thinking:

"Dan, my business is DIFFERENT. I have a _____ (hair studio/ day spa/nail salon/tanning salon/beauty salon."

"That may not work for me"

"My clients are different."

"My town is different."

"We sell based on price."

"I don't really like that. That doesn't really fit me."

There is a common limitation that keeps showing up time and time again with all the hair salons, beauty salons, nail salons, day spas, medi-spas, pet spas, and tanning salons ranging from single-operator salons to full-service spas that I have helped and collaborated with.

The facts speak for themselves. The main limiting factor in taking your salon business to the next level is YOU.

Only you can remove your poisonous thinking that these strategies will not work in your salon. If you hold fast to that thinking, then you will blind yourself to seeing how to implement these strategies in your business.

You didn't pick up this book to learn what you already know, did you? We can all get set in our ways and have a limited view of the world.

Read this book cover to cover and keep an open mind. Then ask yourself these two questions:

- How does this apply to me?

- How can I implement this strategy immediately?

Don't just read this book, use this book. Study the material and apply it. Grab a pen and a highlighter, feel free to write on it, tear it apart, make a mess of it, whatever you want to do – just as long as you use the materials!

By the end of this book, you'll look back on today as the day that changed everything.

Are you ready?

Turn the page.

IT WILL BE A RIDE LIKE YOU HAVE NEVER BEEN ON BEFORE...

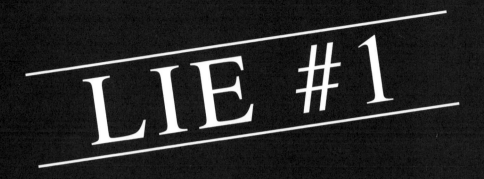

LIE #1

"I JUST NEED TO BE
GOOD AT WHAT I DO,
AND MY BUSINESS WILL
BE SUCCESSFUL."

*"Ye shall know the truth, and the truth
shall set you free." (John 8: 32)*

LIE #1

Do any of these scenarios sound like you or fit your description of yourself as a salon owner?

- Your salon/spa business was supposed to give you financial freedom and independence to do whatever you wanted. Yet it has ended up trapping you into working 50+ hours each week – just to make ends meet. The long hours have physically drained you and prevented you from having a normal life. You miss out on family get-togethers, time with your friends, your children's sports days, dance performances, etc. Even when you do get the chance to go out, you are too exhausted to enjoy the down time. And you feel this way because you're afraid that time away from your business, even if it's for a well-deserved vacation, would spell disaster for it.

- Your salon/spa business hasn't generated the steady income you envisioned to support you and your family. Despite investing tens of thousands of dollars, possibly hundreds of thousands of dollars or even a million dollars or more opening your salon/spa, you don't have a steady stream of clients. Your phone isn't ringing off the hook, your appointment book isn't filled, and your cash register is empty.

- You're financially stressed trying to make ends meet so you can pay your staff and other monthly expenses. You are so sick of struggling, taking all the risks and putting in "sweat equity" that you're about ready to throw in the towel and get a "regular job" with a regular work schedule and regular pay. (You're thinking, "Life was probably quite good as an employee and why did I quit after all?")

- You're doing OK in your business. But other salons and spas have come in and grown faster than yours. The owners are already making the big bucks, driving around in their new cars, living the great lifestyle, going on vacations, while their salon gets packed with clients opening up their wallets to fatten the owners' retirement nest egg. And you're wondering when it's going to be your turn to really live it up.

- You've figured out how to run your salon/spa business – quite successfully. It brings in steady income like clockwork. Yet, somewhere along the way, you've lost that burning desire and passion you once had for your business. Instead of having that skip in your step, you now drag your feet to work. It's become totally boring for you.

- You've had success, maybe even a lot of success and now it's time for expansion. Time to open up multiple locations; acquire some commercial real estate, or maybe even franchise your salon/spa. This transformation is the next step, but you don't know how to go about it.

If you answered yes to any of these questions or can identify and see yourself in any of the above scenarios, then know this:

YOU ARE NOT ALONE!

Although your specific circumstances may be a bit different from other salon owners, you'll probably find the challenges you face are remarkably similar.

Like you, most salon owners were originally hair stylists, salon managers, nail technicians, cosmetic laser technicians, estheticians, makeup artists, or massage therapists, etc.

You have a specific trade and craft you are good at. After all, you did graduate from cosmetology school, receiving the proper and necessary training.

Then you found employment in a salon. Working "hands on" gave you the opportunity to interact with clients, develop your skills, and sharpen your insights to the ins and outs of the beauty industry.

So, after years of apprenticing under your boss, you left the nest and started your own salon.

Good for you.

Now that you are a salon/spa owner, you can call the shots. You can do things your way. But reality sinks in, and you quickly realize what it takes to run a salon/spa business. More specifically, a successful salon business is much harder than it seems.

You know your salon provides great, high-quality services.

You have the best-trained staff with the best equipment.

You have a great location with beautiful décor.

Heck, you could even be the best salon in your area.

Then why aren't you getting what you want from your business?

The truth is…

LOKISM #1

"Being good is not good enough."

BEING THE BEST SALON IS NOT GOOD ENOUGH

We all know this shouldn't be true, but it is.

Many salon owners think that all they need is to be really good and their business will be successful.

The fact is, being a successful salon today has more to do with how you manage and market your salon than it has to do with being the best salon in your area.

Before I continue, I want you to know that whatever situation you are in at the present moment…

IT'S NOT YOUR FAULT

You followed your passion to do what you love.

You got the necessary training and qualifications to do your job.

You give a 100% effort (if not more) in your salon or spa daily.

You have acquired the technical skill and knowledge about your specific area of expertise, meaning you know how to cut/style hair, do a classic pedicure and manicure, apply nail polish, give a massage, facial treatment etc.

But this does not translate into knowing how to run a salon business.

In fact, I am quite sure that when you went to cosmetology school or beauty college for your technical training, you spent weeks, if not months, learning the technical know-how.

I bet there was nothing in the curriculum about how to start and run a successful salon business. And I am not referring to writing a business plan and all that boring stuff.

No one ever showed you how to run, manage, and grow a wildly successful salon business.

I'm taking about practical real-world strategies for:

- ✓ Bringing more high-quality clients through the door.

- ✓ Ensuring your clients return to the salon again and again.

- ✓ Recruiting and retaining the right people to service those clients.

- ✓ Hiring, managing and motivating your team.

- ✓ Selling more retail while the quality of your service remains high.

- ✓ Adding locations and expanding without being stretched too thin.

- ✓ Increasing sales while keeping your costs in check.

So don't blame yourself, OK?

HOW I ACCIDENTALLY BECAME A SALON OWNER

Unlike other salon and spa owners, my journey to becoming the owner of Sweet Nail was purely accidental. I stumbled on this, quite reluctantly, I might say.

As mentioned in the Introduction, I own several businesses.

One day, I came home from a business meeting to find the love of my life, Jennie, in total distress.

When I asked her what was wrong, she looked up at me. It was obvious she had been bawling her eyes out.

She blurted, "I hate school! I hate my food and nutrition class! Why can't I do something I love? I can't stand being stuck in this!"

I asked, "Why are you taking this course then?"

Jennie sobbingly replied, "My parents – they pressured me to take this course even though it's not what I wanted. They believe there's a demand in that industry. They think it is a safe and secure career for me and they want me to graduate."

I said, "Well, why don't you do something else?" as I handed her another Kleenex.

Jennie shook her head, "I can't. There's no way out. You know how much they sacrificed for me so that I could go to college? My family would kill me!"

I persisted, "I completely understand the pressure, but don't let others discourage you from pursuing something you really want to do. It's your life we are talking about, not your family's life."

"Can you honestly tell me," I continued. "That you are prepared to spend the next four years of your life, specializing in an area you have absolutely no interest in, wasting tens of thousands of dollars on tuition, so that you can work at a job that you totally hate, every day for the rest of your life. Is that what I am hearing from you?"

It was absurd to think that was the direction Jennie was heading.

"I don't know…," Jennie muttered as she blew her nose.

I continued, "You're the one that's going to be doing this job every day of your life. Don't do something just to please your parents. I know

LOKISM #2

"Most salon owners don't have, and never develop, the most basic business and marketing skills that will ensure their success."

they only want the best for you, but to be honest, if they want you to be happy, they should let you do what you'd love to do."

I could see Jennie's wheels spinning. Her thoughts were racing across her mind.

"No, I definitely don't want to be doing this for the next four years. If I have it my way, I'd want to do something fun, something related to beauty and fashion, something with nails," Jennie said with excitement.

"Wonderful, that's a start. Why don't you open a nail salon then?" I asked.

"Dan, I could never do that. I don't have the money. I haven't even finished my courses! Where would I go to get the skills to do nails? I have no idea where to start!" Jennie exclaimed.

I'm always eager to help someone I love. So I offered my expertise right away. "Forget the how. The how comes after you decide that it's going to happen. You don't need to know how it will happen. You just need to know why you want it, and decide that is what you want."

"I can help you. I can teach you how to run a business. I can even finance your salon. If you have a strong enough 'why', you will figure out the 'how'. All I need from you is your desire and commitment to see this through from start to finish," I told Jennie.

"Yes! I can commit to doing this," Jennie said.

"Good. Let's look into the future a bit here," I said. "Tell me your vision for your salon. What would make your nail salon different compared to the other nail bars around here? How will it stand out from the competition so clients want to come to your salon? What is your Unique Selling Advantage (USA)?"

"Hmmm...." Jennie paused for a while. "My nail salon would be totally different from a standard nail bar. It will specialize in

LOKISM #3

"You don't need to know how to do something before you do it."

Japanese 3-D nail art. You know, it will look way more elegant, fancy designs with lots of bling. It will transform any plain-looking, boring set of nails into a work of art! Take a look at the design on my nails! They cost me around $150 each visit. There is only one salon in our area that does these types of nails. It's always packed and I have to make my appointment a week in advance."

"Jennie, this is fantastic. Sounds like you may have just stumbled on a niche market," I said.

"What's a niche market?" asked Jennie.

I explained, "A niche market is described as a highly targeted, narrowly focused group of potential clients. A business that focuses on a niche market is addressing a need for a product or service that is not being addressed by mainstream providers. If I understand you correctly, Japanese 3-D nail art is a very specific type of nail service. Clients who are seeking this service will be more than willing to pay premium prices."

"So did I hear you right? That clients pay anywhere from $100, maybe even up to $200 for these Japanese 3-D nails?" I clarified with Jennie.

"Yes," she said.

I continued, "Now let's move on to talk about what you really want out of this business."

Jennie was surprised. "What do you mean what I want out of this business? I just wanted to make a living and support myself."

I hate seeing people start a business for the sake of starting a business. Especially people I love.

"Well" I said, "What kind of a lifestyle do you want your business to provide you?"

"A lifestyle?" she asked.

"Yes, think about the lifestyle you want to lead and then build your business in that direction to support the lifestyle," I said.

It took a bit of time, but Jennie finally came up with her personal list of things that would enable her to lead the lifestyle she wanted.

Jennie's Personal List:	
Personal pampering – hair salon/massage/spa visits ($500 per month)	$ 6,000
Lease car ($800 per month):	$ 9,600
3 exotic vacations per year ($5,000 per vacation),	$15,000
Monthly weekend getaway ($1000, per weekend)	$12,000
Fancy restaurant meals twice a week ($250 per week)	$13,000
Name-brand clothes, shoes and accessories ($1,000 per month)	$12,000
Cleaning service ($200 per week, 50 weeks)	$10,000
Annual gifts for friends/family including Christmas ($400 per month)	$ 4,800
Buy-whatever-I-want money ($1,000 per month)	$12,000
Entertainment, including concerts, theater etc. ($400 per month)	$ 4,800
Charitable donations ($500 per month)	$ 6,000
Personal savings ($1,000 per month)	$12,000
Total:	$117,200 per year

I said, "Jennie, for you to make approximately $120,000 a year, let's pretend our net profit margin is 30%, that would mean your salon needs to generate about $416,000 in gross sales."

"I need how much?" Jennie exclaimed in disbelief. "$416,000! That's a LOT of money. How will I ever make that kind of money?"

"Hang in there," I replied. "This is completely doable. Let me show you." I pulled out my calculator to crunch some numbers.

"OK. We start with breaking this big number down. There are 365 days in a year. Say the salon is open six days a week; that would be 312 days. After public holidays and to keep the math simple, we will base our numbers on plan on 300 working days a year.

"If each client spends an average of $100 each visit, you would only need to bring in 14 clients per day. That is $1,400 a day. Our plan is based on 300 days. When I take the $1400 per day and times it by 300

" Most salon owners never become wealthy because they don't take the time to figure out exactly what they want."

days we get $420,000. See it is possible for us to do $416,000 in sales in one year."

"I don't know," uttered Jennie, still not totally convinced. "Fourteen clients is still a big number to me. It may take a while to get up to 14 clients a day."

I said, "Well, say your salon hires four or five nail technicians, and we aggressively market your salon using some proven marketing methods. Getting 14 clients a day will be pretty easy. Can you see how this is completely do-able?

"It's easy to get completely overwhelmed by the big picture," I said. "The key is to break things down, and work in all the necessary tasks, one step at a time."

"You're right," Jennie responded. "We do this one step at a time and we will get to 14 clients a day. So what we should we do next?"

So after five months of hard work, we opened Sweet Nail.

Using the techniques and strategies that I've learned from my other businesses, Sweet Nail was profitable in our second month.

In the first year, our salon business' gross revenue was almost $350,000 and we took home a profit of around $119,000. That works out to just a little under $10,000 a month. Our net profit margin is running at 34%.

This is phenomenal, because I found out that salon owners bring in only an average of about $35,000 a year. Our nail salon was bringing in $10,000 a month! And our salon is literally brand-new! The success is staggering!

Here's the kicker: Jennie and I have zero experience in the beauty business. We've never gone to beauty college. Neither of us knows a thing about nails. I hate to admit this but I can barely use fingernail clipper on myself!

I rarely set foot in our salon, managing it mostly from my home office. Despite my being physically in our salon for only about three to four hours a week, it runs pretty smoothly.

I know this sounds unbelievable or too good to be true. But I assure you, it's true.

And what made it possible for us accomplish these results?

It is *because* I am not a technician.

It is *because* I didn't know how to – and cannot – do the technical work.

I went into the salon business, really, to help my fiancé. I wanted to see her successful and more important, I wanted to see her happy.

I came in with the mind-set of a business owner, not a worker.

My intention from day one was never to lift a finger to do technical work on clients.

My intention from day one was to build a successful salon business. And I've been able to do this using proven strategies previously used in my other businesses. These are the business strategies and secrets that have worked outside of the beauty industry.

Yes, there are better, more successful ways to manage and market your salon and spa, different than what you've been led to believe.

LOKISM #5

"This is a quality-of-life conversation in business clothing."

THE BIGGEST REASON WHY SALON OWNERS FAIL

What kind of lifestyle do you want from your business? This is the exact question I asked of Jennie when she was ready to commit all her time and energy to start a salon business.

44

And now, I am asking you what you want your life to look like as a result of owning a salon or spa business. Otherwise, why would you start a business in the first place? A business is supposed to support you financially and give you more freedom to do all the things you've always wanted.

From my experience working with salon owners, it's very common for them to say they feel tangled in the day-to-day operations of their salon, often finding it hard to juggle three jobs – one as an owner, one as a manager, and the other as a technician.

To stay on top of things, many salon owners report they spend in excess of 50 hours a week in their salon, trading away their personal time and family time, trading away their sanity – all for the sake of their salon.

The salon that's supposed to give them the entrepreneurial freedom and lifestyle they wanted becomes an all-consuming beast. When they step away, most salon owners are still preoccupied with their business. When they're on vacation, they think about their business. It's with them wherever they go – interfering with their ability to enjoy personal down time, time with their friends, family, and loved ones.

Instead of enjoying their business, owners feel trapped in it. If they are unable to turn things around, many salon owners eventually walk away from their business and lose their life savings.

Another failed business. Another one bites the dust.

What's the cause of these business failures?

I believe too many people get into business for the wrong reasons. They are not happy with their current work environment or are disgruntled with their employer. They want to go out on their own and be their own boss.

Then reality hits them. They quickly learn that they are not their own boss. Instead, their business is the boss. In fact, it's the worst boss they've ever worked for, a slave driver who pays them next to nothing without recognizing their effort.

They get stuck on what I call the Salon Business Treadmill (SBT), working insane hours with little hope for the future success of their business. They have little to no time for themselves or their family. They are caught in a trap and see no way to get out.

---

*"We are boxed in by the boundary
conditions of our thinking."
– Albert Einstein*

WAKE UP!

You need to think about your salon business from a totally different angle.

In order for a business to be emotionally and financially fulfilling for you, you need to first:

- Start out with a goal in mind.

- Decide on the kind of lifestyle you want to lead.

- Decide how you want your business life to be.

- Then start a business and, most importantly,

- Create and structure your salon or spa business in such a way that's emotionally and financially rewarding for you.

It's one thing to make a lot of money. It's another thing to make a lot of money in a way that's pleasing to you, satisfactory to you, physically and emotionally rewarding to you, with clients that are respectful to and appreciative of you, in a way that gives you a lot of control of your time and your life.

So when you're thinking about lifestyle, don't just limit yourself to thinking about a monetary goal.

Remember, you can buy things, but you can rarely buy freedom.

The trick is to know the difference between what is supposed to bring you pleasure and what actually brings you pleasure.

It's about what you really want, not the ideas that the media has sold you on what you should want.

Let me give you a quick example. I have a friend who is a very successful businesswoman. She owns about 75 designer handbags. From Hermès, Chanel, Louis Vuitton, Michael Kors, Burberry, Dior, Prada, you name it, she very likely has it! These handbags cost at least $1,000 each, and as high as $10,000 for a very special handbag.

To accommodate her growing collection of handbags, she even renovated her walk-in closet to add more shelves and cubby space.

But the challenge is, she's stuck in her business, working so many overtime hours, she barely has time to relax, much less take the designer handbags out for a night out.

And to make matters worse, all she can talk about is the next handbag she's going to buy. She's working harder and harder just to buy more handbags that she won't even get to use.

Where is the logic in all of this?

The reason I own my businesses, including my salon, is to generate income so it can allow me the opportunity to do what I really want in life. It's a means to an end.

I can call a friend any time during any given week and say, "How about we do lunch tomorrow, and then go hang out at the beach for a while or go to a movie in the afternoon, go jet skiing, dancing, skiing or sailing, go on scenic plane or helicopter tour of the city, whatever?"

Because of my business success, I now have complete total freedom to live my life the way I want to live it; doing only the things I want to do.

It's all because early in my career, I figured what exactly it is that brings me the greatest joy and pleasure; determined how much pleasure it offers, and what I was willing to pay for it. It all goes back to understanding what makes you tick.

LOKISM #6

"It's not how much money you make; it's how you make the money."

I've discovered that when you've achieved total financial freedom, when you don't have to worry about paying the bills, you can spend most of your time doing the things that bring you the greatest pleasure; like reading a book, spending time with your kids, traveling, having a good conversation with a friend, or volunteering for a worthy cause.

Plus, you can afford to pay almost any price for anything (however, after a certain price point, you're just paying for prestige rather than quality).

HOW TO MAKE ALL YOUR DREAMS A REALITY

To reach your goals, first you have to know what your goals are. You need to have what I call Ideal Life Goals (ILG). Here's an example of what your ILG might look like:

1. Get the car of your dreams.

2. Work in your salon only three days a week and not on weekends.

3. Buy a vacation cabin at the lake that you and your family can enjoy.

4. Take a two-week vacation in Hawaii or Disney World.

5. Pay off your mortgage or buy your first house

When you write out your goals, don't write what you think you can achieve. Write what you want.

Whatever the goals might be, you must calculate what kind of money it takes to get them. You don't think, "Well, I just want to make more money, hopefully". Don't be vague. Calculate how much money you're really talking about.

LOKISM #7

"Too many salon owners live their lives following someone else's agenda."

Without a set of clear numbers, you're sure to get somewhere… but who knows where? If it's your ideal life we want to create, then you're going to need to supply the coordinates.

So here's the assignment: Answer the questions below and take the corresponding actions:

1. Describe the material things that excite you, i.e. things that you often think about and that light you up like a Christmas tree; e.g., travel to exotic places, real estate, bags, clothes, shoes, specific experiences. Make a list of all the items and experiences you want; When would you want to have them over the next year? Be specific, Map out each one and list how much it will cost.

Ex. Family Trip to Disney World, estimated cost $6,000

1. _____

2. _____

3. _____

4. _____

5. _____

6. _____

7. _____

8. _____

9. _____

10. _____

11. _____

12. _____

13. _____

14. _____

15. _____

2. Now total up all the items on your Ideal Life Goals (ILG) list.

_____

The number you get is the amount you would need to earn to each year to support Ideal Life Goals (ILG).

3. Now divide that number by twelve to get what your monthly income needs to be to support your Ideal Life Goals (ILG)?

_____

4. Now that you know what your annual and monthly income needs to be to support your Ideal Life Goals (ILG), are the actual dollar amounts more or less then you thought it would be?

_____

When Jennie added up all her ILG, it totaled about $120,000 a year. That was the cost of her ideal lifestyle.

You might say, "Wow, Dan, that's a lot of money!" and you might be right – it could be a lot of money compared with where you are now. But it's not $5 million or even $1 million, is it? Even if you add some lavish housing with a big mortgage, it's still less money than you think you might need.

My point is this: Most salon owners will realize when they go through this exercise that they actually don't need as much money as they expected to live a happy, rich and fulfilling life.

And isn't that what we ultimately want – happiness and fulfillment?

When I was a poor grocery bagger, my goal was to land a slightly better-paying job so I could support my mom and myself.

> *LOKISM #8*
>
> *"You don't have to know how you're going to get there. But you do need to know where you want to go."*

HOW I DISCOVERED MY NEW LIFE DIRECTION

I am now financially free, which means I never have to work another day in my life if I don't want to. I work because I love what I do. I work when I want, where I want, with whom I want, doing only what I want to do. I make more money in a day working a few hours than I used to earn in six months.

I LOVE my life. I make seven figures a year. I am so grateful every day I am on my knees. I have made a lot of money. I've done a lot of interesting things and met fascinating people. I've traveled to all kinds of beautiful places. I've got friends whom I care deeply about and who care about me.

Out of all the things I am proud of, the one thing that I am most proud of is that for the last five years, I have fully provided for both my mom and my dad so they don't have to work.

I'll confess right now...

Even with all that, I started to get a little bored.

So, I started asking myself, "Is this all there is?" When I was broke, all I did was focus on me and how I was going to become financially free.

Once I became financially free, I started thinking about:

"*What is my life purpose? What I am going to do with the rest of my life? How can I make a difference? How can I give back?*"

Then it came to me, almost unexpectedly.

A couple of months ago, I was at an Italian restaurant having lunch with Jennie. We were laughing and having a good time, when a lady walked up to our table.

"Sorry," she said. "I don't mean to interrupt. You're Dan Lok, right?"

I quickly finished sipping my tea. "Yes, I am," and quickly cleaned my mouth. "Do I know you?"

"You may not remember me," she said. "I'm Christine. I own a salon on Granville Street. I

LOKISM #9

" Let us live our lives AS IF all our dreams have come true, and then challenge reality to catch up."

52

met you when you spoke at a cosmetology school about six months ago. After you finished your presentation, I approached you for some help with my salon. My salon was the one with $50K in debt, and we were about to shut our doors permanently."

"Yes, I recognize you. I remember your situation," I replied.

"Well, I want to tell you that your life story and your salon wisdom really inspired me. It reminded me that once you hit rock bottom [like in my case], you can only climb upward. It gave me hope that I could turn things around. Oh, and those two strategies you suggested, I did use them finally, and started to see positive changes in my salon and more important, positive cash flow coming into my salon," Christine said.

She continued, "If it wasn't for you, I would have given up on my salon dreams. I can't thank you enough for giving me hope and strength to turn my business around. Words can't express my gratitude. Thank you so much."

She kept thanking me and I gave her a hug. A big smile came over my face and I felt a warm glow within in me. There was even a small tear on my cheek.

I had just been given the most profound and incredible gift of my life. I had changed a life.

WOW! What a fantastic feeling!

Jennie reached over, held my hand and said, "Honey, I am so proud of you!"

Then she had this sparkle in her eye and said, "You know, you're really good at running a business. You have the business street smarts – not only book smarts – of what it takes to run a successful business and still have a great quality life. Honestly, I never thought it was possible to make this kind of money in the beauty industry – not until you came along. Our salon – Sweet Nail – would not have become a reality if it wasn't for you."

She continued, "Why don't you start another business to just teach salon owners how to become more successful? You're a great teacher and you're a great mentor. You can relate to all the salon owners. You have this vast amount of knowledge and experience. That is the main reason we have this successful salon business. You can be a role model to thousands of struggling salon owners out there. You can really impact people's lives."

"Jennie, I am not sure. I have too many commitments already. First of all, I don't need the money. I've got other businesses to run. Second, I don't know if I have the time to be this role model for other salon owners. It's a huge commitment. I need to think about it."

We didn't discuss it anymore that day.

Over the next couple of months, Jennie kept pushing, kept requesting, kept nudging me to start a "teaching other salon owners" business.

One day, I went for a walk to clear my head, and then it dawned upon me. I had the big "A-HA" moment.

I said to myself, "I love business and I love teaching. Maybe I do have something to offer to the world. Maybe I can use my gifts to add value to the lives of others."

"No man has ever risen to real stature until he has found that it is finer to serve somebody else than it is to serve himself."
– Woodrow Wilson

ARE YOU WORKING SO HARD, BUT STILL AREN'T GETTING WHAT YOU WANT FROM YOUR SALON/SPA BUSINESS?

I know how you feel. I'm a salon owner myself. I understand the problems you are wrestling with every day.

I also possess the business knowledge that can help struggling salon/spa owners transform their business from struggling to successful.

I am inviting you to take advantage of my knowledge to create a fun, highly profitable salon/spa business that can make your financial dreams a reality.

After long and thoughtful consideration, Jennie and I decided we didn't want to franchise our salon, but our business ideas were too good to keep to ourselves. I accepted and embraced my new life purpose – to build a business around my newfound passion – to share my story and business experience with other salon owners around the world.

And the results were nothing short of stunning.

Those salon owners whom I have had the privilege to serve have told me that I completely opened their eyes to a whole new way of running and growing their business:

- ✓ They are attracting more and better clients.

- ✓ They are working less and making more – even taking a few days off every week.

- ✓ They find lost enthusiasm, pride and joy in running their salon business.

- ✓ They stop arguing and fighting with their partner, spouse, and employees.

✓ They end the day with a sense of real accomplishment, not frustration.

✓ They set exciting goals for their business and achieve them!

I'm truly humbled and honored to be part of it.

That's why I wrote this book. I want to share with you the same proven strategies that have gotten us results so you, too, can experience the incredible transformation in your salon business.

In the next chapter, I am going to show you why most salon businesses don't work and what to do about it.

LIE #2

"THE SALON BUSINESS CAN ONLY BE A GOOD HOBBY BUSINESS OR A LABOR OF LOVE."

"What material success does is provide you with the ability to concentrate on other things that really matter. And that is being able to make a difference, not only in your own life, but in other people's lives."

– Oprah Winfrey

LIE #2

I've got some good news and bad news.

First, the good news.

Running a salon can be one of the absolute best businesses to be in – if you know how to do it right.

I don't mean it's great because you get to be creative, socialize, and have fun making clients, and friends look beautiful, or that you get to do something you truly love.

What I'm saying is that running a salon is great from a business standpoint. I'm referring to:

✓ Dollars and cents.

✓ Profit and loss.

✓ Success and failure.

Let me show you how good the salon business can be in case you're losing your faith. You know you're in a terrific business already.

Just look around. You know there are salons and spas that are still busy and have been steadily growing during the recession. The beauty industry is a $16 billion industry and still growing. As one of my mentors says, "Vanity is here to stay!"

For those of you who like stats and numbers, I will give you just one stat specific to spa industry, though you and I will recognize what is a positive for the spa industry is a positive for the entire beauty industry.

> *According to the International Spa Association, the recession seems to have had little effect on the industry. It reports that the number of spa visits increased 16% and the number of locations rose almost 19%, to 21,300 in the U.S. (Day spas make up almost 80%.) National data also shows that the beauty industry is a $16 billion industry.*

The beauty industry is practically recession-proof.

With the recessionary crisis, more and more people turn to salons and spas to de-stress and relax. They can leave their worries behind with a relaxing massage, a facial, a pedicure. Everyone can use a little pampering in these times.

Lokism #10

"The secret to wealth is committing to one idea over time."

Job seekers still need to look professional for that interview, and when they're out there networking, they definitely want to look sharp. And don't forget, everyone still has significant events in their lives when they want to look great, such as birthdays, wedding, anniversaries, graduations, and reunions. That's when they head to the salon and spa.

IT'S A BUSINESS BASED ON REPEAT BUSINESS.

Industry reports have shown that the beauty industry's growth is based on repeat business. Once clients establish a comfortable working relationship with their esthetician or hair stylist, they generally return to the same person as they want that same quality of service. People in general are very particular about whom they allow to work on their face, hands, feet, body, and hair and will usually return to the same person to get these salon services done. This is a great advantage, as many businesses don't have a repeat-business model.

IT PROVIDES INSTANT GRATIFICATION.

Salons and spas provide a retreat for instant relaxation and rejuvenation. Clients come in to get their nails done, get their backs massaged, get their hair colored – and the results are instant! They leave feeling better about themselves, with a refreshed body and mind, and their natural balance is restored. It's an instant "feel-good" experience every time they come to the salon and spa.

IT'S AN AFFORDABLE LUXURY – A SMALL INDULGENCE.

Salon services are affordable because, for most people, salon and spa services are a small-ticket item. They can justify indulging themselves with a $200 facial treatment, compared to opening their wallets and spending $2,000 to $3,000 on a vacation in Florida or Mexico. It makes economic sense, and is a lot easier to justify psychologically.

THIS SERVICE-BASED INDUSTRY HAS ONE
OF THE LOWEST FAILURE RATES.

A 2007 survey taken by the U.S. Small Business Administration, which guarantees loans for business start-ups, shows that the salon franchise industry has only a 5% failure rate. This is extremely low compared with other service industries, such as restaurants, which have a 10%-15% failure rate.

IT REQUIRES LITTLE INVENTORY OR STOCK.

Retail stores that rely solely 100% on the sale of goods and products for gross revenue, but salon and spa owners do not have this problem. Salons and spas rely on talent and the skill set of their estheticians, stylists, massage therapists, nail technicians, makeup artists, etc. to service their clients. Employees delivering quality service to happy clients are what bring in about 80% of salon revenues. There's no need to carry a substantial line of professional salon products.

Any well-managed salon and spa would adopt a just-in-time inventory model, whereby they carry sufficient products to be used by its staff, for professional display, and for client purchase. It only reorders products just as they are about to run out; therefore, not too much money is put into salon inventory.

The beauty industry has historical roots dating back to ancient Egypt. It has obviously evolved significantly over the years, though the basic services are still the same. Not many industries have such a long and rich history as ours.

Some of the techniques and styles have changed over time, but for the most part, I would say that our industry is here to stay and will still be here a hundred years from now.

The salon business is not based on ever-changing technology. I've talked to owners whose salons are celebrating their 30th year of business. The trends have come and gone over the years, and a few new ones have been added every decade or so, but generally, there is no reason to believe that the salon business will be radically different over the next 30 years from what it is today.

WHY ANYONE – INCLUDING YOU – CAN BE WEALTHY

Running a salon business can be a way to make a lot of money – if you do it right.

A lot of people think that you can only run a salon as a labor of love because you can't really make much money at it.

That's baloney.

I've had the privilege over the last 10 years of learning from and being mentored by extraordinary entrepreneurs, people like Mr. Lai Shiao-Yi, the founder of Mentor Hair.

Mr. Lai started his first salon in 1966, as the Shanghai Mentor Women's Beauty Salon. Lai had learned coiffure from a master hairdresser from Shanghai, hence the company name.

Today, Mentor Hair is one of the biggest chains in Taiwan and has more than 300 locations there, as well as 30 in China and two in Canada.

Does that sound like a hobby or a small business to you?

Another example is John McCormack, the cofounder of Visible Changes. He was originally a New York City police officer-turned-stockbroker who made a million dollars before age 30, and then lost it all.

John's wife owned a hair salon. With a little time on his hands and not really sure how he'd make his comeback, John began pitching in a little around the salon – a few improvements here and then a few more improvements over a short period of time.

Soon, John discovered it could be a profitable business, and felt the industry seemed ripe for innovation. Fifteen years later, Visible Changes is one of the largest and most respected, upscale, hair-salon chains in the United States.

Have you ever heard of Regis Corporation? Maybe not, but it is a Fortune 1000 company and the global leader in salon and hair-care services. Since 1922, it has grown to more than 60 distinct brands of salons (such as Supercuts, Cost Cutters, and First Choice Haircutters), serving 160 million customers annually!

Lokism #11

"If you've hit rock bottom now, don't give up! Very often, you break down before you breakthrough."

So you see, the salon business can be as big, or as small, as you would like it to be.

It can be a nice little business that provides long-term financial security, an incredibly rewarding career and business that allows you to feel that you have made a difference in people's lives and to make people (clients) happy.

Or it can also be a multimillion-dollar empire that will make you richer beyond your wildest dreams.

The choice is yours.

Now the bad news, the salon/spa business can be the absolute worst business to be in if you don't know how to do it right.

It can require you to put in longer hours than you'd like – making you feel trapped.

It can become such a priority in your life that it takes over your leisure activities, your family gatherings, and important milestones. It can take control of your life if you are not careful.

If it's not going well, you can be struggling along, working even harder just to make ends meet, swapping hours for dollars.

But here's the irony:

If you don't know how to set up your salon business properly, you can also become a victim of your own success.

Here's what I mean by that.

DO YOU OWN A JOB INSTEAD OF A BUSINESS?

I've talked to salon owners whose problem was not that they didn't have enough clients. Their problem was that they had too many clients.

One of my coaching students owns a very busy hair salon, and she's one of the best hair stylists in her area. Her problem was that all her clients wanted only her.

Other stylists worked at her salon as well, but most of the clients were referred based mainly on the strength of her personality.

Everyone wanted their hair done by her – and only her.

If they phoned, everyone wanted to talk to her.

If there was a problem at the salon, clients wanted to deal only with her.

In a way, it was flattering, and she did get a lot of Christmas cards from her clients each year. But those Christmas cards came at a high price – a very high price, for that matter.

She told me that some days she felt that clients weren't even giving her a chance to breathe in between appointments. There were days when she didn't have time for lunch. For her to have some sanity and down time, she has to sneak into the back parking lot and sit in her car.

She wanted some coaching from me because she knew she would eventually go crazy if she had to keep up this pace – week in week out, month after month.

She also told me she was worried about cutting back her hours and direct involvement, because most of her success was based on her hairstyling talents and personality.

If you salon is too tied to your personality and your personal skills, your greatest strength can also be your greatest downfall.

ARE YOU GUILTY OF COMMITTING THIS DEADLY SIN?

If you don't know how to set up a salon business that can run successfully without your personal day-to-day involvement, then you don't really have a business.

If your salon business needs you to be there all the time for it to function properly, your salon is not a business – it's a job with hundreds of bosses.

Your salon business can be the worst business if you don't know how to make it run without your direct input.

A lot of salon owners are their businesses. If they don't or can't work, their salon doesn't work, either. If they go on vacation, they are forced to close their doors while they are away. That is one reason many salon owners don't go on vacation. This is a dangerous position to be in.

Ask yourself:

- Do you own your own business or does your business own you?

- Are you building a business that will last, that you can sell or just creating a job for yourself until you retire?

Lokism #12

"The more you personally do in your business, the more you have to keep on doing."

THE MOST COMMON MISTAKES STRUGGLING SALON OWNERS MAKE

I once read an article in a beauty magazine about a salon owner who had a very loyal following. She even had several celebrity clients. One day, she was hit with a bad illness.

She had to close her salon business because she couldn't work anymore. And if she wasn't there, her clients didn't want to come in.

After years of investing her life into her salon, she had no business left and no income.

The medical emergency wiped out her entire savings.

I'm sure a couple of clients wrote her nice cards and bought her flowers and said how much they would miss her, but I'm sure none of them were volunteering to pay her bills each month.

When I first read this article, I felt really sad for her, but then it made me kind of mad.

I knew it didn't have to be that way.

If she had just known how to set up her salon so it could run profitably without her direct input, she could still have a business and an income.

She wouldn't be left out in the cold.

She wouldn't be left with nothing, after building what she thought was a business that was supposed to be more secure – avoiding getting laid off or downsized in an instant – than having a job.

Having a salon can be the worst business if you don't know how to delegate the right tasks to the right people.

If you don't know how to manage and structure your salon business properly, you can end up being responsible for three jobs: a full-time technician with a packed schedule of clients;, a full-time salon operator managing your salon, your staff, office administration, bookkeeping, including payroll, etc., and an owner developing a vision for future growth and deciding what steps are necessary to move toward your business goals.

Are you or do you know salon owners who are literally so consumed by doing every job in the salon that they can't take a day off? Even if these owners could take a day off, they would just end up obsessing about their salon.

And there are other "fires" you need to deal with (just to name a few):

- You can't keep or attract good stylists to work for you or rent a chair from you.

- You don't know how to attract new, quality clients.

Lokism #13

"Profit isn't everything. It's the only thing."

- You are afraid to raise your prices because your long-time clients may go elsewhere.

- Client loyalty isn't what it was years ago because you are losing clients faster than you can get new ones.

- You have lost control of your staff, and you have no idea how to hold them accountable.

- You can't get anyone to sell products (renters or employees)

Owning a salon can be a terrible business if you have to spend a lot of time dealing with customer service issues and putting out fires everyday.

If you, as the owner, have to deal with the same minor, nit-picky details over and over again, it can frustrate you and make you mad, but it can also distract you from doing what you love and running a successful salon.

The emotional burden of having to deal with upset people on a regular basis will cause stress. If this stress keeps building and adding up, week after week, after four to six months you are going to be pretty high-strung and stressed all the time.

If you don't set up your salon business properly, you can make very little money. I know a lot of salon owners who are working like slaves and are still just squeaking by.

WHY YOU DESERVE TO BE FULFILLED AND WEALTHY AT THE SAME TIME

Why get into business if you're not out to make a sizable profit? Who wants to own a business that has cash-flow problems, doesn't allow you to take any time off, and doesn't build long-term financial security for you and your family?

Of course, this business is not just about money.

But it makes no sense for you to provide a valuable service to your community, and still have to struggle to make ends meet.

I believe salon owners who do a good job and provide value to their clients deserve to be well-paid.

I also think you're fooling yourself thinking you should short-change yourself and not get paid for your efforts.

If your clients can afford to pay for your services, they are obviously getting genuine value. There's absolutely nothing wrong with making a profit from your services and feel good about it.

THE ONLY REASON TO BE IN ANY BUSINESS

Let me ask you a question, "Why are you in a business?"

If your answer is "to give me what I want," then you're right!

That's the only reason to have a business, unlike what others want you to believe: the government believes that the purpose of a business is to pay taxes, the unions believe that the purpose of a business is to provide jobs to the community, and some salon owners believe that

Lokism #14

"The sole purpose of a salon/spa business is to give you what you want."

70

the purpose of a business is to provide jobs for themselves and their employees.

Wrong!

The purpose of a business is NOT to provide jobs or support your employees. If you do, that's nice, but that's a side benefit.

The purpose of every business is to give the owner what he or she wants. It's that simple.

If you help people make a living along the way, that's wonderful. But that's NOT the purpose.

The purpose of your salon business is to support YOU – to make you financially independent. That's the only purpose. Period.

BECOME FINANCIALLY FREE AND LIVE YOUR DREAMS

What does financial independence mean to you? How would you feel if you are able to live in the home of your dreams, drive the car that you want, work two or three days a week, go on vacations when you want to places where you have always wanted to relax and have fun?

I believe most salon owners don't get what they want because they don't take the time to plan out exactly what they want. They just know they want something different than what they're getting now!

Remember, clarity leads to power.

Answer the following questions and write down the purpose of owning your salon and what it will allow you to do.

The purpose of owning my salon/spa business is:

_____

_____

_____

_____

_____

My salon/spa business will allow me to:

_____

_____

_____

_____

_____

My salon/spa will allow me to enjoy:

_____

_____

_____

_____

_____

My salon/spa will give me the ability to:

_____

_____

_____

_____

_____

LIE #3

"IT'S A BUSINESS, IT'S
SUPPOSED TO BE HARD
WORK AND LONG HOURS
– IT'LL GET BETTER."

"The secret of business is to know something nobody else does."

*– Aristotle Onassis, one of the world's
richest shipping magnates*

LIE #3

When I was 10 years old, my cousin used to come to my house every day. We'd play games and hang out and do all kinds of fun kid things.

One day, he brought along this odd-looking little toy. It was some kind of straw tube threaded together in diamond-shaped, diagonal patterns.

I was fascinated by it, but I had no idea what it was.

My cousin told me that it was Chinese handcuffs and offered to show me how they worked. He said, "You begin by sticking a finger from each hand into it, and when you try to pull them out... you're trapped."

The thing looked pretty harmless to me. In fact, it looked plain boring. "So how do you get out of it? I asked.

"Oh, don't worry," he said. "You won't have any problems... It's just made out of straw."

Something didn't sound right. I said, "If it's so easy, let me see you do it first."

He put his fingers into the handcuffs, then pulled his hands apart and sure enough, the weave tightened around the two index fingers and he was stuck.

"Now watch this," he said and started wiggling his hands this way and that and until suddenly his index fingers were free.

"Now you try it," he said. "Make sure you put your fingers all the way into the handcuffs to make sure they lock in properly."

I crammed my index fingers in as far as I could, then I tried to pull my hands apart the way I saw my cousin do it. The straw tube gripped my flesh and held my fingers close.

I was surprised – even stunned – at the straw tube's refusal to yield.

The more I struggled, the more firmly the Chinese handcuffs held me. I pulled so hard my knuckles popped, but the straw just dug deeper into my skin. The harder I tried, the worse it got.

I started sweating and my face turned red.

I knew it was possible to break free from the straw tube because I watched my cousin do it. Of course, he was bigger and stronger than me. So I assumed I needed to use more strength and effort to break free.

So I pulled even harder, but still I couldn't break free.

By now, my cousin got tired of seeing me struggle and eventually let me in on the secret. As it turned out, trying harder was the trap.

"Take it easy," he said. "Relax. Now, just push your fingers toward one another instead of trying to pull them out. Give a little twist. Then you can ease your fingers out of the holes."

What he was telling me sounded completely illogical. It didn't make sense to push my fingers into the Chinese handcuffs in order to get them out.

But I was done with pulling at this point.

I was desperate and was starting to lose feeling in my fingers, so I did what he told me.

I pushed my fingers back in the straw tube and VOILA!

My left finger slid out of the straw's clutches and then I slipped the toy off my other finger.

I was amazed at how easy it was to break free when I made the right moves.

A VALUABLE LESSON I LEARNED ABOUT BUILDING BUSINESSES

Running a salon business is similar to the Chinese handcuffs.

You may have been told that you need to work hard to get rich. If you're not rich yet, it's because you are not working hard enough.

So you keep working harder, putting in longer hours, struggling to keep your business afloat, hopelessly waiting for the big payoff.

Well, my friend, I hate to burst the bubble but that's nothing but a **BIG FAT LIE!**

It's a lie that's been perpetuated for generations.

Look around you.

Are there salon owners in your area who are wealthy?

Do these owners work 10 times harder? Are they 10 times smarter? Of course not!

Salon owners who achieve the greatest level of success are not necessarily the hardest workers; they just work smarter with a clear focus, purpose, and end result in mind.

These salon owners have figured a way to build the type of salon/day spa they've always wanted and still have a life.

Lokism #15

"Salon owners who achieve the greatest level of success are not necessarily the hardest workers; they are the smartest workers."

WHY MOST SALON BUSINESSES ARE HARD WORK – IF THEY DON'T MISERABLY FAIL

Let's take a look at the mind-set of a salon owner.

They're people who are independent self-starters and enjoy being in control. They live for the excitement that the salon business can bring them. Moreover, they believe they can do it better than their boss. Does this sound like you?

They see the lifestyle and the money that their boss or other salon owners are making and they mistakenly think that the transition from employee to self-employed can't be too hard.

One of my mentors calls this phenomenon the onset of an "entrepreneurial seizure."

He points out that most people are trained in a technical skill, and they are usually very good at what they do – technically. They may be a good hair stylist, a good esthetician, a good nail technician, a good massage therapist or a good make-up artist, etc.

But having a technical skill set does not qualify you to be a successful salon owner.

In short, technical skills are not equal to business ownership skills. They are totally different.

Too many technicians (employees) suffering from this "entrepreneurial seizure" rush out to open their own businesses by getting a line of credit, using all the equity in their home as security, or investing their life savings.

They invest all their money getting their salon set up and ready to go, hiring lawyers to set up the business and to go over contracts, leasing retail space, decorating and setting up their salon with equipment, work stations, reception area, customer lounge, staff room, computers and other equipment, tools, supplies, and let's not forget the salon signage, logos, letterheads, and business cards.

Lokism #16

"The only thing that can keep you from becoming successful in the salon business is located right between your ears."

They spend a lot of their energy in the set-up phase of their business, but they forget the key element to business success: how to attract clients and keep them coming to their salon.

So when their salon finally opens, salon owners quickly realize that while they have strong technical skills for their specific profession (nails, massages, hair, etc.), they do NOT have the knowledge or experience of running a business.

Getting clients to come to their salon turns out to be a lot more difficult than they assumed. They thought that once their salon was open for business, clients would come.

Well, that's true to some extent.

But without a steady stream of regular clients, a business cannot count on walk-ins to survive – let alone thrive.

Most inexperienced salon owners discover they don't really have a business; they've simply bought themselves a job, and a very tough and expensive job.

Without the specialized marketing skills, they struggle to attract and keep clients. They struggle to pay bills, to pay their employees, to pay their landlord, to pay their regular suppliers.

Reality sets in and the honeymoon is over.

Running a salon business is a specialized skill on its own, which must be learned like any other skill. Unfortunately, it's a skill many neglect to learn before going into salon business.

Lokism #17

"Either make your salon business work for you or you will always have to work for your salon business."

ARE YOU TRAPPED IN YOUR BUSINESS?

Here's a litmus test to see where you stand in relationship to your salon business:

Ask yourself:

" If I were to leave my salon/spa business for two weeks or two months, could it survive and operate without me?"

If you answered "Yes," I congratulate you.

If you answered "No," then what you're essentially saying is that by you being absent for a couple of weeks, your salon business will collapse and you'll end up with no business income.

In other words, you are self-employed, but you don't own your business. It's the other way around – your business owns you.

You operate a business, but you are working harder, putting in longer hours, getting paid less than that you did when you had a steady job with regular hours and regular pay.

Your business owns you – it's got you in a trap and you can't get out.

Or can you?

WHAT TO DO IF YOU WANT TO TURN YOUR SALON/SPA BUSINESS AROUND IMMEDIATELY

Always remember – you have a salon BUSINESS. You don't just own a salon.

To have a thriving salon business, you absolutely must acquire the business and marketing skills essential to building and growing your business.

Just think of the skills you currently possess.

Think of all the classes you took at beauty or cosmetology school. Now consider the things you did as an apprentice. Then add in any specialized workshops or ongoing classes for upgrading your skills. Now add in any kits, tools, textbooks and supplies.

Don't be surprised if you've spent at least $10,000, plus a thousand or more hours just learning your craft and honing your skills to your current level.

Here's the all-important question:

"Since you opened your salon business, how much money and time have you spent acquiring specific knowledge and skills to make your business more profitable?"

How many courses have you taken?

How many books have you bought and read?

How many marketing and business consultants (consultants – not salespeople trying to sell you ads) have you paid for their advice?

Sadly for most salon owners, the answer is usually minimal, maybe $500 – and I am being generous with my estimate. A lot of times, it's ZERO.

A lot of salon owners believe it's acceptable and normal to spend a huge amount of time and money honing their technical skills. Yet, they've NEVER invested ANY real time or money in learning the business and marketing skills required to make their salon business successful.

And people wonder why 80% of businesses fail.

Wake up!

Lokism #18

"Don't just work hard, work hard at working smart."

82

Your technical skills will only get you part way, it's your business skills that will make you truly financially independent in the end.

Think about it this way.

It's like building a state-of-art racecar, and then refusing to spend any money to fill the tank to get it moving and keep it running.

Don't be like other salon owners dooming their business to a life of struggle and hardship. Make a commitment to master the business and marketing skills you need to break free from the trap.

Remember...

NO DECENT BEAUTY OR HAIR PROFESSIONAL WOULD SAY THAT BEING "SELF-TAUGHT" IS A GOOD IDEA

You didn't wake up one day and say to yourself, "I'll just grab a pair of scissors or a nail file and start working on paying clients. I am sure I can figure out the techniques on my own."

No!

You went to the beauty or cosmetology school, took classes and got certified, didn't you?

You realize it's best to learn something from someone who is already doing it. As a professional, you accept this as common knowledge.

You need to apply this same line of thinking to running your salon business!

Don't be fooled thinking you can be self-taught when it comes to running a profitable salon business. A little trial and error here and there will actually cost you more in the long run.

Working harder will NOT solve your problems.

You have to know exactly what to work hard at.

WORK ON YOUR BUSINESS – NOT JUST IN YOUR BUSINESS

Take a look at any thriving business that you encounter, be it a restaurant, a spa, a retail clothing store, or a salon.

These successful businesses have many things in common, but one thing that stands out the most is that their business runs like a well-oiled machine – meaning that several components work together.

The mistake that most salon owners make when starting a salon business is that they treat it more as a hobby, rather than a business.

Most salon owners focus their energy working IN their business, rather than ON their business.

What does that mean?

It means that salon owners spend most of their time taking care of menial tasks necessary, but not always crucial, to the business. They often think along these lines…

"If I hire someone, that's going to put more pressure on my finances. So I'll do all the little stuff for now, and hire someone when my business makes more money."

The result is that the salon owner has created a trap and walked right into it… the trap of being a technician.

But more money might never materialize. Why?

Perhaps the salon owner is now spending more time taking calls, and doing the technical work rather than figuring out new ways to get new clients and grow their business.

The fine line between salon owner and salon slave invariably becomes blurred.

While they may see the bigger picture, they have a harder time separating out those tasks that need to be addressed in order to achieve it.

I know, because I've done this.

In any business, much of the day can be spent focusing on time-consuming, repetitive tasks. Sure, they fill up the day, but what did you really get done?

Have you ever attempted to do the following on your own: greet clients, answer the phone, book and confirm appointments, respond to emails, keep the salon clean, deal with a supplier issue while trying to create a marketing piece, call a printer or local newspaper, decide whether to create and mail out a brochure, postcard or flyer? What should the brochure, postcard or flyer say? Try to update your website? Add a new page or figure out why your website is down?

And don't forget you still have to balance the last two days' salon cash sales, make a bank deposit, calculate employees' payroll checks, reconcile the credit card statement, and meet and talk with your accountant.

Crazy, isn't it?

But how many of us haven't fallen into this trap!

Let's say you had bought a McDonald's franchise. Do you realize that you'd seldom have to step foot in your restaurant to make money?

McDonalds has built its business so that it runs automatically on its own – almost like magic!

> ## Lokism #19
>
> "Build your salon business as if you were going to sell it; you will benefit from a business that runs predictably and efficiently, without being dependent on you."

Instead of you working hours running your McDonalds franchise, you would be automating or delegating everything, probably to high school students who could cook, clean, fry, and take orders better than you ever could, and for minimum wage!

So why do salon owners venture into business thinking that they can do it all?

If your long-term goal is to build a profitable and enjoyable salon business, then understand that you can't do it all on your own!

You might begin by hiring a salon coordinator – someone who will run the day-to-day operations while you address the higher-level issues.

Or you might begin by investing a fraction of that in software that will help you automate tasks. Or you might do both!

Lokism #20

" Jumping around and splashing in the water doesn't mean you are swimming."

WHY REPETITIVE, TIME-CONSUMING TASKS MIGHT BE YOUR DOWNFALL

I used to think that working hard meant filling in every minute with some busy task.

I had to be the master of "efficiency." I was responsible for getting as much done as I could every day and using each day up to the minute.

In my personal life, this would include trying to have breakfast, watching CNN and reading a book. Ask me an hour later what I ate and I couldn't tell you.

Or in my workaday life: how about email? What a fantastic creation! Is there anything else that provides the fulfilling sense of getting things done and staying on top of it than answering email?

I used to check my email 30 times a day and then spend most of the day answering messages. When I got home at the end of the day, I often couldn't recall what exactly I had accomplished for my business, but by golly, I answered a few dozen emails!

At first, I blamed this on the work ethic I learned from my dad as a child. Working hard was a good thing. I was taught: "Work till you drop."

Later, I began to see it as an obsessive-compulsive behavior that dictated how I lived each day and how I felt about each day.

And maybe this need to stay on top of things has turned us all into a nation of multi-taskers. Just think about all the people talking on their cell phones while driving, or worse yet, drinking their Starbucks while talking on the cell phone while driving!

It's nuts!

I was a multi-tasking machine, but the truth is I wasn't really living in the moment. I was just marking items off a list, doing the things that would give me the illusion of moving forward, of achieving my goals.

And it worked, sort of.

I accomplished quite a bit, but I always had this sense of a knife pointing in my back... it never felt as if I was working enough, so I'd only work harder.

And for some reason I wasn't going as far as I thought I would go.

Then I hit a wall.

I went through one of those periods of pure reflection; that's when I began to understand that when it came to my business, staying "busy" was just another way for me to keep from doing some of the tasks that I found unpleasant or dull that were critical to my success.

My moment of truth: I realized that in order to accomplish more, I needed to do less.

MY SUPER-SIMPLE
PRODUCTIVITY SECRET

I observed in my business practice how multi-tasking – being all things to all people – ended up distracting me from the real work that needed to be done.

Immediately, I began to prioritize my day to focus only on a couple of major things that absolutely needed to be completed. By doing this, I not only remained efficient, I was becoming more effective. I finally realized:

"Productivity is maximum results with the least amount of time. Leverage is maximum results with the least amount of effort."

I also began to think about how I should automate certain areas of my business to free up my time and energy to focus on more important issues.

I eventually implemented systems that would help me to delegate and automate tasks and responsibilities.

Whatever system I put into place, I knew it had to do one thing, or it wouldn't be useful: increase my salon revenue, and decrease the amount of work I did.

Think about your day as being made up of nonproductive time vs. productive time.

Earlier I mentioned how, as owners of a salon business, we can easily fall into the trap of thinking that we need to do or oversee everything.

So much of our business appears to be outside of our control that it is only natural that we want direct involvement in all aspects of it.

But such micro management is ultimately wasteful and nonproductive.

Nonproductive activities include talking to your friends, cleaning up, answering phones, scheduling staff, bookkeeping, etc. – activities that don't grow your salon/spa business.

Productive activities include developing new business skills, learning new ways to acquire clients, improving your ads, upselling clients, creating systems, interviewing, hiring and training staff – activities that grow your salon/spa business.

Every day, ask yourself these powerful questions:

1. Is what I am doing now/today the best use of my time?

_____

_____

_____

2. What is the most important thing for me to accomplish today? The second and third most important things?

_____

_____

_____

3. Are the meetings, appointments and reminders on my calendar today directly related to revenue generation?

_____

_____

_____

4. How can we work smarter, not harder?

_____

_____

_____

5. Who else has gotten the results I want, and what can I learn from them?

_____

_____

_____

6. What resources are we overlooking or under-utilizing?

_____

_____

_____

7. What processes within my business are under-performing?

_____

_____

_____

8. What past or current relationships could I more fully leverage (i.e. clients, employees, vendors, suppliers, advisers, etc.)?

_____

_____

_____

9. What technology could I utilize to automate aspects of my business that are time-consuming and repetitive?

_____

_____

_____

10. What other industries could provide me with some innovative outside-of-the-box ideas?

_____

_____

_____

11. Where are the hidden profits and customer-service opportunities within my business?

_____

_____

_____

TO RECAP THIS SECTION:

- Commit to developing your business and marketing skills.

- Work ON your business, not just IN your business.

- Delegate and automate, so your business runs efficiently and smoothly.

Remember, the goal isn't to have a salon business that you have to work in each day, but to have a salon business that allows you to live an extraordinary life.

In the next chapter, I am going to teach you a marketing system that really works, to attract all the good clients you need.

LIE #4

"WE JUST NEED TO GET OUR NAME OUT THERE."

"Marketing and innovation produce results; all the rest are costs. Marketing is the distinguishing, unique function of the business."

– Peter Drucker, leading management guru

LIE #4

- Are you sick and tired of wasting money on advertising that gets minimal results?

- Are you tired of riding the financial roller coaster, where sometimes your appointment book is overflowing with a wait list and sometimes it's empty as a desert?

- Have you ever wished you knew a proven, cost-effective marketing system that really worked, and produced a steady flow of new clients consistently?

If you answered "YES" to one or more of these questions, then this chapter will open your eyes to what marketing and advertising are really all about.

WHAT ADVERTISING SALES REPS DON'T WANT YOU TO KNOW

Lokism #21

"Your ad doesn't need to get your name out. Your ad needs to get your clients in the door."

You often hear people say that for your salon business to survive and thrive, you need to get your name out there and build a brand for your business, so it can stand out among your competition.

WRONG!

" Brand awareness is absolutely worthless unless it leads to sales."

In fact, brand-name recognition is just an over-hyped, over-priced lie that has led salon owners, just like you, to waste hard-earned dollars on advertising concepts that don't work. It's one of the biggest mistakes I see salon owners make.

You see, your ad doesn't need to get your name out there. Your ad needs to get your clients in the door.

"The sole purpose of marketing is to get more people to buy more of your product or your service, more often, for more money. That's the only reason to spend a single dime."
– Sergio Zyman, former chief marketing officer of Coca-Cola

All media reps, newspaper, online sales and Yellow Pages sales reps are highly persuasive on the topic of brand-name recognition or awareness.

This is their bread-and-butter strategy, where they convince you that the reason you don't have enough clients in your salon is that no one knows your salon even exists.

Brand-name recognition is absolutely worthless unless it leads to sales.

Understand this simple fact: Advertising sales reps are paid based on how much new business they bring in for their company.

So the more money they get you to spend, the more money they make.

They are more concerned about making money for themselves and less concerned about your ad generating new business or profits for your salon.

Advertising sales reps are also keen to use the "frequency" and "repetition" cards as part of their persuasion strategy to get to you spend more money with them.

They often tell salon owners that your business needs more exposure. And the way to get exposure is to keep running your ads, over and over again. The more often you run your ads, the more exposure your salon/spa gets. And people need to keep seeing your ads over and over again before they respond.

They tell you to be patient. It's all about repetition.

No, it's not about repetition. It's about the end results. If your ad is ineffective, it doesn't matter how many times you repeat it.

Think about it.

Lokism #23

"Marketing is math."

If you're trying to reach someone but have the wrong phone number, will dialing the same number five more times make a difference? NO! It doesn't matter how many times you dial the number, you still won't get to the person you originally intended to reach – because it's the wrong number to begin with!

Bottom line: Don't listen to sales reps' advice to repeat your ad bookings (not even if they offer you a frequency discount) unless the ads are successful in bringing in new clients. Only repeat successful marketing campaigns – not the ones that flop!

A third sneaky sales tactic commonly used by media sales reps is the "bigger is better" strategy, i.e., Increase your ad size so your clients can notice you.

If your ad isn't drawing enough attention from people, they say, it's because it's too small. They tell you to enlarge your ad size, so more

DAN'S CHILDHOOD YEARS

My grandma used to dress me up in pink or light blue like a girl. Until this day, I still don't know why. I am amazed that I haven't had an "identity" crisis. My grandma and Mother say I was all happy.

At age three, drinking my milk at a family picnic. I still drink milk to this day.

I come from a large family with so many uncles and aunts that I lose track of most of them. Family is one of my core values. I am the one holding the gun in the front row on the left.

DAN'S CHILDHOOD YEARS

I love Superheroes. I used to think that only people with special powers could be heroes. Now I realize everyone can be a hero. A hero simply means a servant to many. Anyone who's giving back to their community is a true hero in my book.

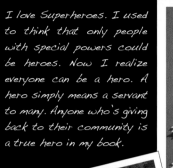

5 years old, posing for the camera. Can you tell that one day I would be sharing the stage with Robert and Kim Kiyosaki, Julie Morgenstern and George Foreman? I have come a long way."

6 years old, celebrating my birthday at my Kindergarten school. Boy, did I love cake!

One of my many travel adventures with Mom and Dad.

DAN'S TEENAGE YEARS

Mother and son moment. Everything I am, I owe to my Dear Mother. Without her, I would be nothing.

Age 10, clowning around at Ocean Park in Hong Kong.

Eighteen, and pretending to be Bruce Lee with one of my friends. At the time, I thought I would open up a martial art school and be an instructor for the rest of my life. I guess I have always had a passion for teaching.

My love of martial arts was my training ground for developing confidence, self-discipline and focus which I later used to become successful in the business world.

Dan's Salon - Sweet Nail
During Renovation

Renovating was a tiring and painful process, Jennie and I
were determined to push through until we were done.
It was a mess. Never give up!

Renovating is dirty hard work. Unbelievable how filthy the bathroom was. I
don't want to think about that ever again.
Trust me.

Sweet Nail Today

Outside looking from the sidewalk, the front entrance to our salon Sweet Nail.

Sweet Nail's comfortable and spacious waiting area.

Our custom designed nail stations. "Let the pampering begin".

Dan - The Proud Salon Owner

It's possible to create a business that you can be proud of while at the same time provide a great lifestyle for you and your family with the proper knowledge and systems in place.

It wasn't always smooth sailing. Just like you, we had to conquer all sorts of challenges to become successful. 3 days after a flood to our salon we are still using industrial strength fans to blow dry the floor and the walls.

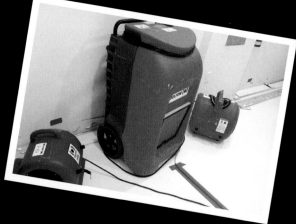

Dan's Mission & Passion

Me sharing my business success lessons and secrets with 350 or so business owners.

I love to share my story!

Getting ready to give another one of my signature presentations. I get very intense and passionate when I teach.

79 happy clients from one of my premium coaching groups ready to apply all the practical street smart knowledge in their business.

DAN HAS ARRIVED

Me and my dream car – Audi R8. I love driving this car! A former college dropout, I transformed myself from a grocery bagger in a local supermarket to a multi-millionaire.
I am the perfect example of " Whatever your mind can conceive, and you believe, you can achieve."

I know if I can do it, you can too! Let me show you how to create an abundant, joyful and prosperous business and life.

"No man has ever risen to real stature until he has found that it is finer to serve somebody else than it is to serve himself."

~ Woodrow Wilson

people will notice it. They tell salon owners, "Don't change the copy or ad design, just make the ad bigger!"

This thinking is ridiculous!

It's the same as a waiter saying, "Madam, you don't like the pie? Why don't you try a bigger piece?"

Frequency and size sound like logical reasons for why people respond to advertising, but the truth is neither frequency nor ad size will make any difference. Not if the ad doesn't work.

For example: In your daily commute, you drive by a restaurant twice a day – once to work, and once back from work. You obviously know this restaurant exists because you've seen its sign more than 1,000 times.

But you have not set foot in that restaurant, let alone eaten there.

This example clearly shows that brand name recognition has nothing to do with increasing sales. Brand-name recognition helps to confirm that your business exists, but it is insufficient to count on it to get paying clients through your salon doors.

AN EASY WAY TO ADOPT THE MINDSET OF SUCCESSFUL AND WEALTHY SALON OWNERS

Running a profitable salon is really just math. To really determine the effectiveness of your marketing dollars, you need to crunch some numbers – do the math.

Let's say a typical client spends an average of $100 each time she visits your salon. *(I know your actual price may be higher or lower, but let's keep it simple with $100.)*

If you have 100 clients paying you $100 per visit, that's revenue of $10,000 a month. Let's say you have $5,000 worth of operational expenses each month: rent, staff, product, and other standard overhead such as phones, heat, electricity, etc.

$10,000 minus $5,000 leaves you with $5,000 gross profit – that's if you're the sole proprietor or operator.

Now let's say instead of 100 visits, you have 300 clients paying you $100 visit per month. That's $30,000 in gross sales.

You obviously have incurred more expenses to accommodate 300 clients. You are likely to have more equipment, more staff, and a manager working for you to service the larger client base. Let's estimate these expenses come in around $15,000 per month.

$30,000 - $15,000 = $15,000 per month in profit.

That's a net of $180,000 per year.

Your numbers may be different as far as what you charge and what you pay out but the bottom line is: If you want to make more money, you have to know how to *attract* and *keep* more clients in your salon.

HOW TO DOUBLE OR TRIPLE YOUR SALON PROFITS

Most salon owners are really confused about what marketing actually is. Many of them believe marketing is just doing some sort of advertising to promote their salon.

You have to realize that advertising is just a small part of the process. There's a whole lot more to marketing than just advertising.

Most salon owners do not have a reliable, consistent new-client attraction system, nor do they know how to create one, let alone do any effective marketing at all. And I don't blame them. Most salon owners simply don't have the tools to correctly attract clients nor do they have the time to learn how to do the right things.

You've probably tried doing some traditional advertising here and there. Maybe you've even tried advertising your salon or spa in various other ways. Or maybe you have tried advertising in the paper, Yellow Pages, or flyers,

Most likely, you were rarely successful. Why? Because it's not just where you advertise, but how you advertise that determines your results.

When I ask salon owners if they've heard of using postcard mailings or direct mail, they often tell me that they don't use postcards or direct mail because it's too expensive and "it doesn't work."

Really?

I've used postcards and direct mail to promote Sweet Nail, and I'm getting $35.31 back for every $1 I spend, I think direct mail works great. Why does one type of advertising work for one salon and not another?

The reality is: If you don't to know how to use something, it probably won't work.

This is a good time to introduce you to …

BRAND-IMAGE ADVERTISING VS. PROMOTIONAL ADVERTISING

All advertising can be broken into two major categories: brand image and promotional.

The first type is commonly known as institutional advertising or branding. This is commonly taught in many business schools and colleges.

It is predominantly used by banks, insurance companies, and most big corporations. You've seen many examples of image advertising. It may have someone's logo or company name, maybe a clever slogan.

In their printed or online ads, you can see that they use certain positive images of the company to convey key messages to its audience.

It attempts to tell how great the company is, that it is trustworthy/reliable and better than its competition.

It attempts to give the company a look of professionalism.

It attempts to make the prospects feel good about the company. And the focus of brand-image advertising seems to be "me" advertising.

Image ads perpetuate the false belief that if we look really good on the outside, then people are somehow going to be compelled to do business with us.

Think of your ad as your salesperson. Would you hire a salesperson to get a sale by contacting your prospective clients and just saying the company name over and over? Calling them on the phone, whispering your business's name, and hanging up?

You wouldn't send a door-to-door salesperson to someone's home to hold up a sign with your company name and logo and say, "Hi, I've been in business for 20 years. I have a pretty logo, look at me, aren't we great? Oh, you may have heard our name."

You would expect a lot more than that from a salesperson. Then why wouldn't you expect just as much from your ad as well?

Brand-image advertising makes sense for Kraft, Coca-Cola, Nike, and Sony. Huge companies have to spend money on that kind of advertising to keep their names out there in the commercial world. The idea is that when people make buying decisions, they will favor products whose names they know.

Brand-name consumer products almost always outsell generic products. Trust comes from familiarity, and familiarity increases sales. The problem is, it is very, very expensive to

Lokism #25

"The goal is selling, not just running promotions."

create a household name. We are talking about tens of millions or even hundreds of millions of dollars.

Brand-building is for patient people with very deep pockets. That's probably not us.

But if you are a salon owner working with a limited budget, then focus on response and sales. If you develop brand recognition as a by-product, great. But do not spend money exclusively on creating it.

Promotional advertising (also known as call-to-action advertising) is designed to get prospects to respond to your ad immediately (by picking up the phone or walking in) so you can measure the results of your promotion.

Promotional advertising uses four main elements to engage the prospects. In printed or online ads, you can usually see an enticing offer, sufficient information about the product or service being offered, an explicit "call to action," and finally, a means of response such as a phone number, a website or specific webpage.

Unfortunately, for most salons, the extent of their "advertising" efforts is nothing more than a blown-up version of their business card.

Their salon ads typically have a logo and a nice picture of their salon, or a pretty face, and surrounding these images is info about the salon "This is who we are, this is what we do, and here's our phone number."

Classic brand-image advertising.

There's a very high probability that prospective clients glancing over these salon ads will not call and make an appointment. Why? Because prospective clients need to be given a reason to come to your salon. They are thinking, "So what?" or "What's in it for me?" or "Why should I make an appointment?"

A good ad should have a powerful benefit that captures the attention of your target audience. It overcomes objections, answers questions your prospects might have, it promises results, and makes a compelling offer for them to respond – now.

Don't just tell your prospects about your salon. Sell them on the benefits of coming to your salon. Give them a reason to contact you.

Keep in mind, an ad is going to cost you the same amount of money if you get one call or if you get 100 calls, so make your ad message count.

FOUR IMPORTANT RULES OF PROMOTIONAL ADVERTISING

✓ **Rule #1:** Never do anything that doesn't let you directly track its results.

✓ **Rule #2:** Never run an ad a second time if it didn't work the first time.

✓ **Rule #3:** Never fall in love with your ad.

✓ **Rule #4:** Never listen to anybody unless they can market better than you.

You may love an ad, you may think it's a winner; you may think it is the greatest ad you've ever designed. You run it, and it fails. Don't continue running it because you think it's great or because it's got your picture on it. Don't fall in love with your ad. Results rule. Period. Opinions don't count; only results. If an ad doesn't fill your appointment book, stop it.

And one more thing: Time after time, I've seen a perfectly good ad being discarded because someone close to my students said, Oh, I would never read that many words", or "That's not pretty enough."

This is an important piece of advice: Don't listen to anyone who hasn't proved to you they can market their business better than you can.

It's better to just test the ad – let the results speak for themselves.

Until you test your ad, anything that other people say is irrelevant, unless they are a proven marketer making lots of money in their salon business.

Now that you fully understand the two types of advertising, and how advertising is just part of the marketing process, it's time to talk about what marketing is all about.

Before I continue, let me first tell you…

WHAT REAL MARKETING IS NOT

Sometimes, knowing what NOT to do is as important as knowing what to do.

- Real Marketing is NOT getting your name out there.

- Real Marketing is NOT name recognition.

- Real Marketing is NOT building an image.

- Real Marketing is NOT getting your name in front of as many people as you can.

- Real Marketing is NOT bragging about how excellent you are.

- Real Marketing is NOT copying Fortune 500 companies' cutesy or funny marketing.

- Real Marketing is NOT cold-prospecting.

- Real Marketing is NOT begging people for referrals.

- Real Marketing is NOT going to network meetings and social events to meet clients and prospects.

- Real Marketing is NOT having a brochure and business card. It's not even being very good at what you do.

- Real Marketing is NOT winning an award. It's not having letters after your name or a beauty college degree.

- And finally, Real Marketing is NOT hoping and praying for clients to call you. It's NOT pretending to have a predictable income stream from referrals only.

WHAT REAL MARKETING REALLY IS

Real Marketing engages a diversified group of systems that automatically deliver ideal clients to your salon in a predictable manner.

Ideal clients are described as those who are pre-interested, pre-motivated, pre-qualified to pay higher, premium prices. They will also happily refer their friends and family to your salon.

These systems run on autopilot and don't require active manual labor on your part.

You don't want to be running around looking for prospective clients. You want to structure your marketing so that they automatically come to you.

With a Real Marketing system, you will no longer have to worry where you next client will come from. You no longer have to worry about keeping your staff busy at times. And you no longer have to worry about covering payroll, rent, and other recurring expenses.

Lokism #26

"Hope is not a strategy."

This is what a Real Marketing system can do for you.

Ask yourself:

- Do you know the lifetime value of your existing clients? Yes or No

- Do you know how much it costs to acquire a new client for your salon? Yes or No

- Do you have a marketing system in place to attract new clients? Yes or No

- Do you know where your best clients come from? Yes or No

- Do you have trackable marketing systems in place? Yes or No

- Do you know what your return on investment is for every marketing dollar you spend? Yes or No

- Is your marketing system a one dimensional approach or is it a marketing system: multifaceted, strategic, incorporating online and offline combinations? Yes or No

If you answer "No" to these questions, you're guaranteed to be disappointed with your marketing results.

Lokism #27

"Think of marketing is an investment, not an expense."

LOOK OVER DAN'S SHOULDER: HOW I USE THE INTERNET TO DOMINATE MY LOCAL MARKET AND BEAT A COMPETITOR WITH MULTIPLE LOCATIONS

When Sweet Nail opened its doors, I knew we were in for a challenge. The area where my salon is located is surrounded by lots of competitors. One of them, Pure Nail Bar, is a highly established business with 10 locations.

I knew I had to do something different. I knew, with Sweet Nail being brand-new to the area, that I needed to work on building a client base – *almost immediately.*

During our salon renovations, I started working on our website and getting it optimized for Google.

Google is the dominant search engine in the world, so submitting my website to Google is imperative for my online presence. Specifically, I wanted to get my business listed in the Google Places feature (previously known as Google Local Listings).

At this pre-launch phase, all my website had was a basic home page that built up excitement and buzz around the pending launch of Sweet Nail and to invite people opt-in with their name, phone number and email address, giving us permission to contact them when the Grand Opening happened.

So even before we opened our doors, we already compiled a waiting list of customers eager to come to our salon.

Sweet Nail is listed in Google Places. As you can see, when people type "richmond nail salon" in the search box of Google.ca, Sweet Nail comes up first.

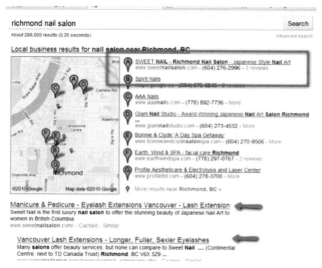

Even if people type in "Vancouver nail salon," Sweet Nail still dominates the listing!

I personally trained my team to promote my websites. I've been able to dominate my local market and beat out my competition.

My competitor, Pure Nail Bar, has 10 locations and has been in business way longer than we have, yet Sweet Nail is still able to outrank them in Google.

What if you are ranked #1 in Google in your area, do you think your phone will ring off the hook? You bet.

Here's what's really profound. In the mind of potential clients, perception is reality. If you're ranked as #1 in Google, you must be good. (At least Google thinks you are good.)

Even though we were brand-new and hadn't even opened yet, being #1 in Google has given Sweet Nail instant credibility. It feels as if we've been in business for a long time. It feels as if we're a really good nail salon.

Positive expectations lead to positive outcomes. Then all we have to do is fulfill their perception through providing them exceptional service to turn that perception into reality. And that's exactly what we did.

Today, 60% of Sweet Nail's new clients come from the internet.

And my team does an excellent job in keeping us in the highly coveted #1 position in Google.

A NEW WAY OF GETTING CLIENTS THAT REALLY WORKS

One of the most widely used social networks of this decade is Facebook.

Facebook now has more than 500 million active users and is growing every day. That is about one person for every 14 in the world. It has an amazing power to connect people from all over the world.

Sweet Nail has a Facebook page, for the purpose of connecting with our existing clients, as well as to showcase the type of service we provide at our nail salon.

We frequently update our photos page with pictures of the latest nail designs we've worked on. We have nail photos for special occasions like Christmas, Valentine's Day, Halloween, and other holidays.

It has an Info tab as well, so prospective clients can visit our website and see what we are all about. They can even contact us for an appointment.

One of the features I like about Facebook is the Like button, which is located next to the business name.

People who visit this page on Facebook, can choose to click on this button if they like what they see. And this is a very powerful endorsement tool, it's a viral testimony that they support your business, and there it is again, instant credibility.

Check out my Facebook page at www.facebook.com/sweetnail to see all the Sweet Nail fans.

There's no doubt Facebook has definitely helped us grow our salon business.

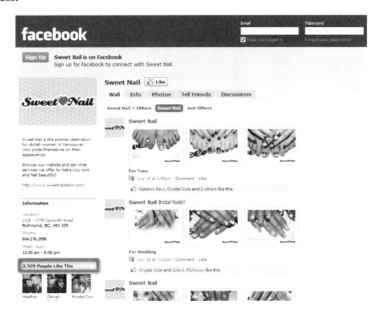

THE QUICKEST, EASIEST AND BEST WAY TO GET A NEVER-ENDING SUPPLY OF CLIENTS

Ask yourself:

When prospective clients look for a salon in their area, how do they go about finding one? Where do they turn?

Common answers to this question are:

- The Yellow Pages

- Community newspapers

- Hair and beauty magazines

While it's true that these are all very common methods of finding local businesses across all industries, there is one place where more and more potential clients are searching for places to spend their money: the Internet.

In fact, using the Internet has outnumbered traditional search methods considerably. And the growth of online search methods is showing no signs of ever slowing down!

In fact, it's safe to say that for prospective clients under the age of 40 today…

If they can't find you online, you don't exist.

So when your prospects go searching, will they find you? Or are you like most other salons, lost on the web? Or worst yet, would they find your competition before they find you?

I truly believe the Internet is the most reliable, predictable and consistent way of bringing new, quality clients to your salon. Love it or hate it, you need to stay on top of the expanding digital economy if you want a thriving salon/spa business.

FEELING FRUSTRATED AND OVERWHELMED? NEED MY HELP?

I've just given you a sneak peek of how I've leveraged the power of the Internet making Sweet Nail the No. 1 nail salon in both the Vancouver and Richmond areas. I even beat out my local competitor who has multiple listings.

And from first-hand experience, let me tell you: Even the best salon or spa in the world will struggle and suffer, even go broke, if you're not correctly and consistently attracting new clients on a regular basis. Walk-ins and word-of-mouth aren't going to cut it. What you need is a guaranteed, predictable marketing program that brings you new clients consistently, every day, week and month.

Many of the salon and spa owners I talk to tell me about the pain and frustration they've had over the past few years trying to make their online marketing efforts work.

Many also complain how costly it's been. Some have paid huge amounts of money, much of it wasted on a poor-performing website that gets them no clients.

Many just don't have the time and energy to keep up with all the marketing and social media they know they should be doing. They need a way to fill their appointment books to capacity, quickly and consistently, without spending hours upon hours marketing themselves.

Others have told me they don't have a website, but want to get it right the first time and not waste any money on something that just won't work.

That's why I've created a powerful and effective solution for salon or spa owners just like you that will give you the online and social media presence you need to fill your appointment book quickly and consistently without you spending hours and days doing all the work yourself.

It's everything I do for my business, but in this case it's my handpicked team working for you and with you, to help you attract more clients using my proven online marketing strategies so you can dominate your local market.

However, we don't take on everybody that applies. You have to prove to me that you're ready to take action, that you're serious and passionate about achieving success.

This exclusive program is NOT for those who are in hairdressing or beauty therapy as a hobby. This is only for serious business people who want to increase the value of their salon, make more money, and enjoy a profitable and stress-free business.

To apply or get updates regarding the done-for-you marketing program, make sure you sign up for my complimentary free online video training at www.salonbusinessexpert.com.

Also don't forget to become a Salon Business Expert Facebook fan by going to www.facebook.com/salonbusinessexpert.

LIE #5

"IF ONLY I COULD GET MORE CLIENTS IN THE DOOR, MY BUSINESS WILL BE SUCCESSFUL..."

"There is only one boss. The customer. And he can fire everybody in the company from the chairman on down, simply by spending his money somewhere else."

– Sam Walton, founder of Wal-Mart

LIE #5

Once upon a time, there was an African farmer who heard many stories about other farmers who had made millions discovering diamond mines.

This farmer was so excited about the possible riches he could have that he sold his farm and spent the remainder of his life prospecting all over the continent in search of these high-priced gems.

Unfortunately, after many years of unsuccessful searching – and in a fit of despair – he threw himself into a river and drowned.

In the meantime, the buyer of his farm was getting adjusted to being a proud owner of a new farm and its daily routines.

One day, he crossed a small stream on the estate when suddenly a flash of blue-and-red light caught his eye. Curious, he bent down, put his hand into the water and pulled out a fair-sized stone.

"What a great looking, shiny crystal! It'll be a great addition to the fireplace mantel," he said to himself. So he took it home and didn't think more of it.

A number of weeks passed.

One day, the new farmer had a visitor. When the visitor walked inside the farmer's home, he saw the stone above the fireplace. He picked it up, pulled out his magnifying glass and examined closely.

He nearly fainted! The visitor asked the farmer if he knew what he had found. The farmer replied that he thought it was a pretty piece of crystal.

Lokism #29

"Clients are the source of your wealth."

116

The visitor told him that it was actually the biggest uncut diamond he had ever seen!

The farmer then told the visitor that his stream was actually full of such stones – though not as large as this one – but there was a large sprinkling of them all over the stream bed.

As it turned out, the new farmer owned one of the most productive diamond mines across the whole of Africa.

Remember the first farmer who drowned himself in desperation? Little did he know that he already owned acres of diamonds.

If only that first farmer had taken the time to learn about what diamonds looked like in their natural state, and then surveyed his property BEFORE starting to look elsewhere, all of his wildest dreams would have come true.

That's how you should view your salon business…

You already have an acre of diamonds –
they're your existing clients.

THE SINGLE MOST IMPORTANT ASSET IN YOUR BUSINESS

In today's competitive marketplace, it is essential for all salon or spa businesses (big or small) to hold on to their single most important asset — their existing clients.

Most salon owners are far too focused on getting the next client while neglecting and ignore their existing clients.

Remember, there are competing salons trying to steal your clients every single day. Your clients are being bombarded by their advertising and marketing. They are trying to steal the equity in your business and steal money from you. They are trying to put you out of business.

To win this battle, it is critical that your salon business creates long-lasting relationships with your clients.

To do this, you must first start cultivating and nurturing a client list.

UNCOVER THE HIDDEN PROFITS IN YOUR BUSINESS TODAY

Too many salon businesses spend most of their time chasing after new clients while neglecting their existing loyal clients.

This is like going out on a great date and at end of the night, you kiss your date and say you had a wonderful time. You'd love to see him or her again but you don't get around to reconnecting for a second date until four or five months later.

That's just way too long. You'd lose your date forever! You would never do that and expect to get another date with that person.

It sounds ridiculous, yet many salon owners treat their existing clients the same way – like a lousy, one-time date

DID YOU KNOW?

✓ It is far easier and cheaper to get an existing client to come back to your salon than to attract a new one.

✓ In fact it is five to six times more expensive to get a new client to come to your salon than to sell services to an existing client.

✓ More importantly, studies and surveys have shown that clients who have visited your salon even just once; will spend, on average, twice as much as first-time clients.

(Source: Various, including the Luxury Institute and the National Association of Retailers)

You will always make more profit from continuous, ongoing client relationships than from occasional one-time walk-ins.

Stop chasing new clients if you're neglecting your existing clients.

The *hidden profit* is with your long-time loyal clients. Once you focus on nurturing your clients and building a loyal fan base, your salon/spa business will begin to flourish.

Question: What are three things that you can do to deepen your relationship with your existing clients?

_____

_____

_____

_____

HOW TO KEEP YOUR CURRENT CLIENTS COMING BACK AGAIN AND AGAIN

How do you start a client list? It's fairly easy.

But I am frankly surprised how few salon owners have a client list, let alone a client list with proper contact information.

I mean a client list with more than just a name and a phone number. Some salon owners have some email addresses. Many have client information written on 3-by-5 cards or scrap notes, backs of envelopes etc. Many times you can't read their email addresses or other important information.

You need to respect your client list and enter it into some kind of database or salon software. Your client list is the source of your profits and wealth. It's like Al Pacino in the movie Scent of a Woman. I always loved the quote "Nurture it, protect it and it will make you proud,'" because the key to your business is your client list.

119

Lokism #30

"Your client base is the most valuable asset your salon has."

Your salon's single greatest asset is not your skill, it's not your location, and it's not even your team of employees. It's your client database.

It's not your client's job to remember to visit your salon, it's is your job to remind your client.

The main reason you gather the information from your clients is to keep in touch and strengthen relationships with them. You need to collect the bare minimums including:

1. Complete name

2. Complete address

3. Phone number

4. Email address

If you are prepared to take the next step in information-gathering, go ahead and collect details such as:

1. Purchase history /purchase habits (i.e. do they come to the salon every month, what do type of services and products do they purchase?)

2. Date of birth or (at least) birth month

This list of information is the critical building block to establishing and building client relationships so you can market your salon to them and generate profits.

Wealthy salon owners understand the riches are in mining their own client base. And they have a system to keep in regular contact with their clients.

Do you have a system?

THE TWO ESSENTIAL INGREDIENTS OF A THRIVING SALON BUSINESS

Let's clarify the difference between a *strategy* and a *system*.

A *strategy* is a method or a technique used to create immediate or short-term profits or cash. Some examples of strategies include running an ad in your local paper, or printing a bunch of flyers and putting them on car windshields at a local mall.

A *system* goes beyond strategies. The best way to explain the power of systems is an acronym:

S – Save
Y – Your
S – Self
T – Time
E – Energy
M – Money

Lokism #31

"Struggling salon owners get a client to make a sale. Wealthy salon owners make a sale to get a client."

- A system helps you create cash or profits beyond an emergency, one-time basis.

- A system can bring in new clients on a regular basis and, more important, it can keep those same clients coming back over and over again, year after year.

- A system can help you and your staff be more focused on implementing strategies.

- A system is a process that produces results that are, (1) predictable, (2) consistent, and (3) replicable – meaning that they work the same way, over and over, and produce the same results every time.

- A system can virtually run on autopilot, without you, even while you're on vacation.

To be a wealthy salon owner, you must both implement strategies and establish systems in your business.

If all you ever do is random, spur-of-the-moment, emergency-cash, one-time promotional strategies, you will always feel frustrated and trapped in your business.

My goal is to help you establish business systems that work continuously bringing in cash on a regular basis, day after day. Allowing you, the salon owner to finally achieve real freedom to enjoy life more and pursue the passionate work that compelled you to go into business in the first place. You can then pursue new aspects of the business you couldn't get to before.

An entirely new world awaits your business once you have established systems that attract quality clients, captures their contact information and communicates with them automatically.

Let me take you behind the scenes and walk you through the step-by-step system we use at Sweet Nail.

STEP # 1: COLLECT THE CONTACT DETAILS OF ALL SWEET NAIL CLIENTS

Every new client who comes into my salon is acknowledged and greeted within three seconds by my smiling receptionist, who says, "Welcome to Sweet Nail, How can I help you?"

Once my receptionist gets the name of the client, she automatically knows whether she is a Sweet Nail member or not.

If the client is not, the receptionist automatically enrolls her into our free membership program called Sweet Members.

Sweet Nail is strictly a members-only salon. I want my clients to get the message that as soon as they walk in the door of my salon they are going to have a unique and special experience. They are not just another random customer. They are our members. This makes them feel important and special.

And with membership comes a bunch of privileges.

Just enrolling them as a Sweet Nail Member separates us from all the other salons. It puts Sweet Nail in a much higher social status – automatically.

The process of becoming a Sweet Nail member is real easy and takes less than two minutes. My receptionist only has to enter 10 fields of basic information. She has a short, casual conservation with the client while she enters the information.

In my Membership Enrolment Form (see next page), you will notice that we don't just get an email address and a phone number. We also collect their mailing address and their birthday month.

One more thing: It is important to get specific permission to contact your clients. Notice the wording I use at the bottom of the application form, that's clearly visible with a large font size.

Here is my exact wording:

Providing this information constitutes my permission for the exclusive use of Sweet Nail to contact me regarding related information via email, text message, fax and phone.

Membership
Enrollment Form

Sweet Nail invites you to enroll as a Sweet Member today and begin enjoying the exclusive benefits immediately.

What Are the Benefits?

♥ *Sweet Benefit* #1

When it is time for a new nail set, nail removal is included free for Sweet Members. (A $25.00 value)

♥ *Sweet Benefit* #2

That's not all, light up your birthday month with even more surprises from Sweet Nail. Simply present your Sweet Nail Birthday Postcard (which you'll get in the mail) to enjoy fabulous discounts!

Simply complete the form below:.

First Name: _____ Last Name: _____

Primary Email: _____

Address: _____

City: _____ Province: _____

Postal Code: _____ Date of Birth (Month/Day): _____

Cell Phone: _____ Home Phone: _____

Signature: _____

(Providing this information constitutes my permission for the exclusive use of Sweet Nail to contact me regarding related information via email, text message, fax and phone.)

Now that we've collected the client's information, we move on to the next step.

STEP # 2: KEEP IN TOUCH WITH SWEET NAIL MEMBERS VIA EMAIL AND OTHER MEDIA

Most salon owners do a truly terrible job of following up and staying in touch with their clients. They view it as an expense of operations – while I view it as "marketing." I believe you should spend at least as much time per year on retaining your clients as you did on getting those clients in the first place, if not more.

My goal is to "touch" each of my clients 24 times a year with a phone call, an email, a Thank You card, a customer appreciation event or some kind of seasonal mailing, like a letter or a postcard that they receive at their home. I know how important is to have them visit my salon again, especially within 30 days of their initial visit.

If I can get one of my new clients to come into my salon two to three times in the first 60 to 90 days of visiting my salon, there is a very high probability they will become Sweet Nail clients for a long time.

Because I understand and apply this principle, I send all of my new clients a "Welcome Letter" within the first few weeks of their first visit.

One of my favorite strategies is the client's birthday month.

On the client's birthday month, I send out a personalized birthday card with a gift from Sweet Nail. Because people rarely receive any personalized mailings from a local retail store or from any other salon, they are ECSTATIC when they receive our birthday card. It makes our clients feel really special.

They rave about this to my staff when they come into the salon. Our clients are excited about their birthday gift, thank my staff, and even more important is they tell all their friends about the great gift they received from Sweet Nail.

SIX POWERFUL REASONS WHY YOU SHOULD LAUNCH A LOYALTY PROGRAM

As you can see from my Sweet Nail Membership Enrolment form, we collect 10 basic fields of information.

Technical details aside, this very simple, two minute enrollment process kick-starts the cycle for the rest of my Loyalty Program. Without this critical information I could not contact my clients by email, phone or mail. Keeping in touch with my clients on all kinds of special occasions strengthens and deepens our relationship.

Lokism #32

"Don't delegate when you can automate."

Using this Loyalty Program, Sweet Nail clients are not just any type of clients. They are exclusive Sweet Nail members.

And this process of turning them from regular clients into exclusive members has ensured that my top Platinum Sweet Members spend between $2,000 and $3,000 a year with me.

Every dollar I invest in my Sweet Nail Members pays me back 10-fold or more. They are worth the investment.

Here are six powerful reasons your salon or spa business should have a loyalty program:

1. Members of businesses with loyalty programs typically spend at least twice as much as those of similar businesses without them. This means that you don't need a lot of clients to make more money. Fewer clients are fine, but you need to use systems to effectively cultivate their loyalty to your salon.

2. Members of businesses with loyalty programs typically patronize the business more frequently than nonmembers.

And members typically refer more of their friends to the business more frequently, too.

3. Creating a loyalty program differentiates your salon business from other salons. It creates the perception that your salon is "not just any salon," that it is somehow better than the rest. That immediately puts your salon into a higher class. And in a client's mind, perception is reality, and a more favorable perception means a more favorable reality.

4. Loyalty programs provide you with an environment conducive to selling more of your salon products and services. It is common knowledge that businesses with loyalty programs sell more products/services and at a higher price than businesses without loyalty programs. Sweet Nail is the classic example. From their first welcome letter to ongoing special mailings and emails, Sweet Nail has a reason to contact our clients, telling them about special promotions, events and offers that we are having.

5. Loyalty programs can stabilize your cash flow. No more riding the roller coaster where one week your cash register is super busy, and the next it's so dead-quiet that you can hear a pin drop. With a loyalty program, you no longer have to wait for clients to come in, or worry about seasonal down time. Your clients will be coming in regularly, and creating a solid, predictable income for you.

6. Loyalty programs can make your salon business more valuable and more saleable. Most salons can provide historical data on sales and income numbers, but struggle to show future predictable monthly income that will come to the salon.

When you implement a loyalty program, it ensures a continuous income stream for you. The Loyalty Program I use in Sweet Nail is so sophisticated it even generates a bunch of current and projected reports so I can – quite literally – predict my salon income for any month! Just imagine what this could mean when the time comes for you to sell your salon, it's a great negotiating tool to have!

I'll say it again: The gold is in your existing clients. Never underestimate what a loyalty program can do for your business. It can transform your business with amazing speed and ease.

PLUG THE HOLE IN THE BOTTOM OF YOUR INCOME BUCKET

Despite understanding the powerful impact of a loyalty program, many struggling salon owners are still resistant. You might be saying, "But Dan, a loyalty program sounds like a lot of work."

The main concern being the amount of additional time, workload and cost to get the loyalty program off the ground.

Yes, it's a lot of work. And I used to dread the idea of having to create and operate a loyalty program myself.

It could take years and cost tens of thousands of dollars just to figure out the right combinations to make a loyalty program run like clockwork.

I almost gave up on the whole thing,

Then I found a loyalty program that does it all and more!

And my whole perception of loyalty programs totally changed 180 degrees.

I now use a loyalty program that works for all salons and spas – big or small.

It even has an extensive reporting capability – which is extremely important. It helps you measure the results of all your marketing campaigns and allows you to check at a push of a button the health of your salon business.

I occasionally have salon owners say to me, "Dan, it's too expensive to have a loyalty program and to send mailings to my clients."

If you can't or won't invest $5 to $10 a year per client to stay connected with them, what are you spending your marketing dollars on? Even if you could not directly trace a dollar in sales to this, you must do it just for client retention.

But, while you may not measure your lost clients who have been wandering off or being attracted by another salon, you can measure the return on this investment, and almost every salon owner who does ranks it as their best marketing investment.

Not having a loyalty program is 10 times more costly than having one. *Don't step over dollars to pick up dimes.*

You may recall that when Jennie and I opened Sweet Nail, our goal was to have 16 clients a day, which would generate an average of $1,600 day in gross sales, with a goal of $32,000 a month in gross sales.

From Day One, using a rewards program, I was able to create reports for everything:

- Total number of Sweet Members
- Total Sweet Member visits per day
- Total Sweet Member sign-ups By month
- Top 10% of Sweet Members by dollars spent
- Top 10% of Sweet Members by visit frequency
- Top percentage of clients by visit frequency
- 100 best clients
- Client visits per day

- Gross sales by day

- Gross sales by week

- Gross sales by month

- Gross sales year-to date

- Sweet Members with birthdays next month

- Sweet Members who have not visited salon in last 90 days

- Etc. Etc. Etc.

Now that I am using a loyalty program, and profiting from the steady flow of income from my existing clients, I can never go back.

Sending promotions including mailings to my Sweet Nail members every month is a lot more effective and cheaper than having to go out and get new clients. I see the value of retaining existing clients, and nurturing them.

"A 5% increase in customer retention yields profit increases of 25-100%."
– Frederick Reichheld, author of The Loyalty Effect

Lokism #33

" The more data you have about your client, the more prosperous your business will become."

MORE PROFIT – MORE TIME OFF – FEWER HASSLES

I recently consulted with a spa owner with a million dollar business eager to get to $1.5 million. I quickly identified the places in her existing client base (of about 9,000) that the additional $500,000 already existed. This is not at all unusual. In fact, it's common. There's

130

usually enough readily available opportunity to increase a salon/spa business' sales by at least 50% without getting even one single new customer.

Ask yourself: When was the last time you received some kind of postcard or letter mailing from a local retail store? You probably can't remember, because it almost never happens.

By keeping in touch with my existing clients, I am keeping Sweet Nail fresh in their minds. I am reaching out to them, cultivating and building an ongoing relationship with them. They are valuable clients.

I show my clients I care about them, and that I'm prepared to invest in them and go the extra mile to get their business. I've automatically set my business apart from my competition. Specifically, that Sweet Nail is above the competition.

Lokism #34

"You can't improve what you don't measure."

Once you have systems in place, you can create an unshakeable personal bond with your ideal clients 24/7 (on autopilot), provide above-and-beyond customer service, crush your competition, and create true wealth in your salon business.

Just think:

- How much *less stressed* you would be when new clients appear at the click of a button.

- How *much easier* your life will be when your clients spend twice as much.

- How *much more fun* you will have when your loyalty program runs itself.

- How *much more freedom* you would have to enjoy time with your family, friends and hobbies.

Look into investing in a proven loyalty program immediately – you can't afford NOT to.

If you want me to recommend the right software that can automate these tasks for your salon or spa, email my office at support@ salonbusinessexpert.com.

Lokism #35

"You are in the relation-ship business, not the beauty business."

LIE #6

"I HAVE TO LOWER MY PRICES TO BEAT OUT MY COMPETITION."

"Live by price, die by price."

— DJ Richoux, salon marketing expert

LIE #6

It's Thursday, 9:20 a.m. It's quiet, and you can feel the energy creeping out of the room.

Simone, one of my high-level, group-coaching clients, is on the proverbial hot seat.

She owns Chester Hair Salon on Chester Street, a small boutique salon with five employees, situated in a growing family-oriented neighborhood. She's been a coaching client for the past year or so.

Simone is looking down; she doesn't want everyone to see her wet eyes.

After a long pause, Simone says "My salon's in trouble. I should have done what you suggested at our last group-coaching meeting, then I wouldn't be stuck in this awful situation."

Chester Hair Salon was Simone's dream. Having apprenticed for years as an assistant, working her way up from junior stylist to master stylist, Simone knew she had found her passion. She knew how to cut great hair, which kept her clients happy, and they kept coming back to her – over and over again.

After years of saving up her money, working long hours, and losing weekends with her family and friends, she finally had enough to start her own hair salon. It was right on Chester Street, where she grew up and had so many fond memories of her childhood and youth.

As I look into the faces of other coaching clients, I know there are other salon owners in the group experiencing the same problems and challenges as Simone. As I am coaching her, I want to teach everyone a lesson.

"Simone, take your time. Tell me what's going on. How can I help you?" I ask, as I try to calm her down.

"Dan, my salon is struggling -- big time. I've been falling behind on my bills for more than nine months now. I'm looking at close to $45K in the hole. My credit cards and line of credit are maxed out. I've been using them to pay my rent, stylists, product, heat and electricity – just to keep the place running. I barely have enough to take home for myself.

"A couple of months ago, I did the credit card bounce-around thing. You know, using one credit card to pay the other off. I couldn't make ends meet. Now the credit card companies are calling. And I'm running out of excuses to tell them. I've used everything from my car needing unexpected mechanical repairs to my husband losing his job. Soon I'm going to have to take money out of my retirement fund and maybe even my daughter's college fund."

I don't want to sound too direct. But I have to know.

"The last time we chatted in person was at your grand opening. Things were going great. How did you go from such a high to this now?" I ask.

"The grand opening... that was an unforgettable day. I did everything you suggested in our group-coaching session. It was PERFECT!" Simone sighs. "I wish I could turn back the clock to that day!"

It had been indeed a perfect day. Chester Hair Salon was bustling with excitement. Simone successfully implemented various marketing strate-

Lokism #36

"Most salon owners under-value themselves, their services, their products; poorly package and present those things; and under-estimate what their clients will pay."

gies I shared with her, and the end result spoke for itself. Her small boutique salon was packed with about 30 clients, fresh faces, people she hadn't met before. She was a little nervous and awkward at first, but I encouraged Simone to work with the local business owners beside and around her salon to promote the big day.

Simone was no longer a salon apprentice – working for somebody else. She was finally the salon owner. It was a proud moment for her.

But the honeymoon phase quickly passed according to Simone. "After the grand opening, I got new business fairly quickly, and many of them were referrals. So I knew our quality was high and clients were happy. Our appointment book was pretty packed daily through to the weekend. Our stylists were busy. Money was coming in steadily. I was seeing some profits fairly quickly. I can't say what happened exactly… but things sort of flattened out in our fifth month. It was getting harder to keep the stylists busy. Chairs were not being filled – even on the typical days. I hated seeing white space in our appointment book. I didn't know what went wrong. All I knew was I needed more regular clients. And I couldn't count on walk-ins."

She continues, "So I started looking around, checking out my competition. I drove by their parking lot and it seemed like there were a lot more cars in their parking spaces. I even casually walked by their salon to check them out. And their chairs were pretty full. Their stylists were busy!"

"I thought to myself… Whatever they are doing to get more business must be working," Simone sounds really convinced. "From what I could see, the real difference between their salon and mine was their prices. They were offering discounts left, right and center."

"Dan, I wanted more business. I needed more business. I needed it so badly I could taste it. Naturally, I jumped on the bandwagon and started offering discounts too. Color your hair and a get a free haircut.

Back-to-school $6.99 haircuts for kids. Cut your hair and get a deep conditioning treatment at 15% off. Monday special 20% off."

I ask, "And did you get any clients from these promotions?"

"I got some extra clients that way," Simone admits. "But it wasn't enough to break even. I know I am providing better service than my competition. And my hair stylists are better trained. I just don't understand why I am not doing better. If I could just break even, it would keep my creditors off my back, and at least give me a fighting chance," Simone was sure about this.

THE MOST IMPORTANT LESSON I HAVE LEARNED ABOUT PRICING

This is a typical situation I have encountered with several of my coaching clients.

Many struggling salon owners are barely making enough to make ends meet. Oddly enough, they think that they are pricing themselves out of the market. And believe they need to lower their prices so they stay competitive, and this is the way to bring in more clients. In their minds, lowering prices will give them a fighting chance.

I have one thing to say at this point...

"That's nonsense!"

I compare struggling salons to a luxury cruise liner maneuvering the rough waters, waves crashing in from all sides, but still holding on.

When a struggling salon starts lowering their prices, it's like the same luxury cruise liner hitting a big iceberg puncturing a big hole in its side. Slowly but surely, water fills the ship. Like the Titanic, down she goes.

It's sad to see many salon business owners getting trapped on the low-price path, when they could be charging a lot more money using a proper system that teaches them how to deal with pricing their services so they don't just stay competitive – but they also make a healthy profit.

"Simone, if you want a fighting chance – a real fighting chance – you're going to have to deal with the price issue," I say.

"Dan, what should I do?" she asks.

HOW TO GO FROM THE BOTTOM OF THE LADDER STRAIGHT TO THE TOP

"I am still new to this business. Chester Hair Salon has only been in business for a little over a year. We're still establishing ourselves in this area. And it's a growing area – lots of potential with many new families moving into the area, I don't really think that price is what's causing my financial challenges and woes," Simone continues.

"I feel I have to do the time, pay my dues before seeing some sort of payoff financially in this business. I was told I shouldn't expect to make a profit for at least two years. That I should just be patient and not be greedy. Things come to those who work hard and wait," Simone adamantly protests.

"What dues?" I ask. "You're making the classic mistake many salon owners make. All price resistance is in the mind of the salon owner, not of the client."

Simone is confused. "I don't really understand what price resistance means. Dan, I recall you mentioning that at the seminar. I don't think this concept really sunk in for me. Can you please elaborate?" she asks.

I am more than happy to elaborate. "Price-cutting is a self-inflicted wound. Your competitors do not lower your prices, your clients do not lower them. You do it. You come up with

Lokism #37

"All price resistance is in the mind of the salon owner, not of the client."

Lokism #38

"*Salon/spa business is a game of margins, not volume.*"

the price, you publish it, and you put it in your advertisement.

"If your competition's prices are lower than yours, that is their problem, not yours. You're the one who tells the printer what to print on your price sheets. If you're not happy with the price you're charging, then change it. Don't complain that your clients only want low prices or that your competitors are forcing you to lower your prices.

"Most salon owners, especially those new to the business, are fearful about pricing," I continue. "They don't want to seem over the top, so they naturally take the middle-ground approach, more often than not, pricing their services a little lower than the competition, believing this strategy will increase and retain their client base. In their minds, they charge what they think clients will perceive as 'too much,' they will lose business and drive their clients into their competition's waiting lap. This is just not a smart way to set prices."

"Dan, what do you suggest I do?" Simone eagerly asks.

I am on a roll at this point. I explain, "You have to be able to price your service in a manner that people are going to want to pay for it. The formula for how much you charge for something is based on your ability to sell it."

She can't believe her ears. "You mean… I don't have to care what my competitors are charging?"

"That's exactly right," I answer. "And the more you learn about selling your services and products and how to promote and market your salon and how to create a buzz about your salon, the more you can charge for your services. It's as simple as that."

I ask everyone to write this down: "If you want to sell to high-end clients and charge premium prices, you need to ramp up your level of service and the quality of your staff. The solution is to charge more money, so that you can make more money, so that you can deliver a better experience."

WE CAN MAKE IT UP IN VOLUME

This is another big lie that salon owners buy into. They think, "I'm going to keep my prices low and I'm going to make it up in volume."

And Simone is no different in this regard.

So I ask her. "Simone, do you know exactly how much gross sales you need to make to break even in a day, a week? And what your profit margin needs to be? You know, stay on the green side of things?"

It suddenly gets silent.

After waiting for more than a minute I say, "Simone? Are you with us?" I know this is a touchy subject, but I have to get to the root of the situation.

"No, Dan, I can't say I really know," she replies quietly. I can feel her mind drawing blanks at this point.

And I feel sorry for her. Many salon owners are in the same boat as Simone.

"Don't feel bad," I say. "A lot of salon owners don't know or understand how much their net profit is. They run their salons based on their gross sales and they brag about it as if that's some big deal; when in reality, the only thing that really matters when you're looking at your financial statement, is how much money you're putting in the bank, a.k.a. NET PROFIT. The truth is – volume does not matter as much as net profit."

ASSIGNMENT: SERVICE AS YOUR
COMPETITIVE ADVANTAGE

Reflect back on a time when you cut your prices to "be competitive." What happened? What was the experience like? Did the client really appreciate the discount, or did he or she feel they "got what they paid for." Did you enjoy the work?

_____

_____

_____

_____

Now think of a time when you may have charged a higher premium than you were used to. What was that experience like?

_____

_____

_____

_____

You want to have the type of client who you enjoy working with, where you can deliver the type of value you want to deliver and get paid well for it.

HOW I POSITION MY BUSINESS TO CHARGE ABOVE-AVERAGE PRICES

When I started Sweet Nail, it was under the most undesirable circumstances. It was during the recession, when people lost their jobs. Our local sales tax jumped from a manageable 5% to a whopping fat 12%. (Blame the government on this one!) And the salon was located in a city flooded with dozens of competitors.

Under these circumstances, you would think the odds of my business succeeding are pretty low.

Guess what I did?

I threw traditional thinking out the door. Instead of low-balling my services, I strategically positioned my salon as a luxury, high-end salon.

It would be one of most expensive, if not the most expensive, salon in my area.

Sweet Nail uses the best products, hires the best employees, and we offer an experience unmatched by our competitors. It would be the "Jimmy Choo" salon of my city.

Why did I do it this way? Why did I go against conventional thinking? To do one thing:

ELIMINATE AND REPEL BARGAIN-PRICING CLIENTS

Truth be told, everyone is a price shopper in some areas of their life.

But, in other areas, price is completely irrelevant.

When I was a "starving" college student, I scrimped by living on instant noodles, but I paid top dollar for a haircut and hair coloring. (*I was trying to get a date – I knew my priorities!*)

I know people who complain about fuel prices as they drive their Mercedes to get a $5 venti latte.

I know people who won't pay $50 for a massage, but will drop thousands of dollars on a laser skin treatment.

If it's something they don't care about – paper towels, for example – they will buy the cheapest option.

Lokism #39

"You'll become effective only by being selective."

144

If it's something they appreciate and value, such as their only child's college education, then they will seek the best over the cheapest.

Bottom line: If people highly perceive the value of an item, the cost of the item itself does not become an issue. The value outweighs the cost. In fact, it doesn't even have to be true value; perceived value is sufficient to outweigh the item's cost.

Makes sense, doesn't it?

At Sweet Nail, people call from time to time inquiring about our prices.

"You charge how much?" the price shopper complains over the phone. "That's crazy, I can get the same service for half that from the salon round the corner from you... I'm afraid I'll have to go there!"

Yes, they often compare us to the competition.

Sometimes, I just can't help but find myself laughing out loud at those people who threaten to go with one of my cheapest-price competitors.

Lokism #40

" People afford what they want to afford."

I think to myself, go ahead and get it done down the street for a cheap price. I am in business to actually provide value and live a lifestyle and make a profit. And if I can't do that with that person, I am just not going to have her as a client.

Conventional wisdom would say that our competitors should have all the business in my city and we would be left with none.

But that is not the case.

Sweet Nail continues to grow, even as our price increases along with our quality of care and service. We are booked solid two weeks in advance, and we constantly have to turn clients away.

And my competitors? One of them just went out of business.

> *"If you don't have a point of difference, you'd better have a low price."*
> — Jack Trout, best-selling author of Marketing Warfare

WHAT REALLY MATTERS TO YOUR CLIENTS

Price is defined as how much something costs.

Value is what you get in relation to what you paid for.

If you lower your prices to beat out your competitors, your competitors will simply lower their prices again. You don't want to get into a price war with any of your competitors. You will both lose.

Remember, the more you lower your price, the public perception is: *"It's too good to be true. Surely, there must be something wrong with the service."*

It may seem counter intuitive; but when you raise your prices, people will deem it more valuable. Most people have a perception that the more expensive something is, the better it is.

Lokism #41

"Stop discounting prices and start adding value."

146

It's much easier to sell at premium prices when the value and experience are greater than the price.

You need to actually package your salon services and show to your clients that the value and experience you are providing far exceed the price.

When you are building value for your clients, you need to remember at all times that…

Lokism #42

"Low prices attract disloyal, unfaithful clients, clients you can't build a business on."

YOU ARE NOT YOUR CLIENT

There's a danger in evaluating through you own eyes what services and prices you should have, because you're NOT your client.

Someone who knows all the ins and outs of housecleaning could – with a little elbow grease – clean their own home.

But someone like me – who hates housecleaning and does not want anything to do with it – would be ecstatic to hire a cleaning service to have this all taken care of.

In fact, I value my time so much I will pay $50 an hour to a cleaning service to gain three hours of free time.

You need to realize that you are not your own client. A lot of us have clients who actually have a better lifestyle and make more money than we do. One of the myths salon owners believe is, "I wouldn't pay that $120 for a particular service, so I certainly can't charge $120 for that service in my salon."

WRONG!

Right away, when you raise your prices, compared with your bargain-priced competitor, you automatically attract a different type of client.

Low prices attract the price shopper always looking for bargains. They will negotiate till they're blue in the face to get the lowest price.

Premium prices attract a loyal, long-term client who's willing to pay a higher price to get what she wants.

Increasing prices enable you to attract a completely different market of clients. No question about this.

HIGH PRICES = BETTER CLIENTS

"Simone, I hope you are starting to realize there are clients out there who are willing and able to pay premium prices for quality services," I say.

"The key is for Chester Hair Salon to put the right system in place, so you can attract and build relationships with ideal clients who are willing to pay top dollar for your top quality work and services."

I continue, "Believe me, your life as a salon owner will be so much easier when you attract the right type of clients. Just think, instead of your salon working hard to convince a client she needs your services, your salon coordinator is now booking multiple services with the client."

"Yes, Dan," Simone says. "I am starting to see your point."

So I ask, "Tell me, what is Chester Hair Salon doing right now to get clients? Do you have a consistent and proven marketing system to do this?"

"Not really." Simone admits, almost in embarrassment. The only marketing she's done since the grand opening was offering discounts – one too many!

"I briefly covered this topic in the past." I say. "Have you heard about 'push' marketing strategy?"

"Yes, I think I heard you mention this before."

This is an interesting topic. "Most salon owners adopt a push marketing strategy instead of a pull marketing strategy. In a push marketing system, the message is sent out in all directions, trying to push anyone they can to do business with them. The glaring message being received is that the salon owner needs clients more than the clients need the services; and this is a bad position to be in," I explain.

"If you position your salon correctly with a pull marketing system, you pull the clients into your salon. Think of this strategy as a magnet. Here, they are seeking you out, and all you need to do is extend your hand and lead them in, pull them through your salon door. In a pull marketing system, clients are seeking an expert, a problem solver in YOU. The positioning is obvious: The clients need you more than you need them."

Ka-ching!

Simone is excited to hear this. "Dan, how do I get my hands on this pull marketing you are referring to? It sounds like it can really pull me out of my troubled waters now."

"Well, first, you need to identify your ideal client," I reply.

HOW TO IDENTIFY YOUR IDEAL CLIENT

The quality of your business is directly related to the quality of your clients.

This is why it is important to define who your ideal client is. If I were to ask you, "What kind of a life partner do you want?" you wouldn't reply, "Anyone that breathes." Would you?

No, you would tell me in detail exactly who you are looking for. Maybe you would say, "I would like him to have a great personality and sense of humor. He should be kind, loyal,

Lokism #43

"The quality of your business is directly related to the quality of your clients."

honest, loving, sincere, affectionate, and caring. He should also possess the qualities of maturity, integrity, and generosity.

"My ideal mate would be a wonderful partner. He should be able to openly communicate his thoughts and feelings and share everything that is important to him with me..."

Then why should it be any different in your salon?

Life is too short to take on just any client.

If I can suggest, one of the absolute, must-have criteria is that all of your clients must respect your team.

Respect is a big thing in any industry. When you allow your clients to walk all over you or your employees, you not only become incapable of commanding respect, but you also become incapable of commanding high prices.

In Sweet Nail, I've empowered my team in such a way that if one of my clients crosses the line in words or actions, they have permission to fire the client. It doesn't matter who they are or how much they spend. And the same goes for my stylists; I expect them to show the same kind of respect to the clients.

Ask yourself:

1. What type of clients can I serve best?

2. What type of clients need what I offer?

3. What does my perfect client like?

4. Where is my perfect client base?

ASSIGNMENT: YOUR IDEAL CLIENT

Write down the qualities of your ideal client. Include things such as how much they pay for your service, their attitude, and other qualities.

_____

_____

_____

_____

"WOW! That's amazing," Simone blurts. "I don't think I've ever thought about my business in those ways."

"It's all about taking one step at a time," I say. "So far, I've shared with you how important is to set higher prices to separate yourself from your competition. But there's another element that can also set you apart from your competitors. And that's…

CREATING THE RIGHT EXPERIENCE FOR YOUR CLIENTS

Well, the fastest way to get out of the lowest-price trap is to create an experience that makes the client feel valued and appreciated. Those feelings are in short supply in the world today, and people will pay for an experience.

Think about the Apple company.

They are a very interesting business case study. Apple does not participate in the electronic market of computers and music players. Apple designs products that speak to the desires and tastes of their clients. Apple creates experiences and moments for their customers.

People do not own a computer – they own a Mac. They don't own an "MP3 player – they own an iPod. They don't just own a cell phone – they own an iPhone.

Apple has created its own culture, its own language, its own attention to detail and support that surpasses anything its competition has to offer.

It doesn't really have competitors, because the experience and products are unique compared with what similar companies offer.

And, because of this, it is able to charge very high prices, and customers are happy to pay them.

In fact, customers line up to buy Apple products and don't feel they are overpaying.

It's an apples and oranges comparison (or Apple and PC). It's simply not the same product.

Lokism #44

"Don't sell services, sell experience."

In the salon business, the quickest way out of the low-prices trap is to stop being like every other salon. Stop doing the same things every other salon does – doing the same services, charging the same prices.

In your salon, don't sell services, sell experience. People will always pay a premium price for a better experience.

Position your salon as if it's a cut above all other salons. By doing this, you will attract clients who want what you have to offer.

Ask yourself:

1. How can I increase this level of perception?

2. How can I increase this level of service?

3. How can I increase this level of experience?

ASSIGNMENT: RAISE YOUR STANDARDS

Are there times when you service could have been better? When?

_____

_____

_____

_____

_____

Brainstorm some ways you can "wow" your clients. What are some things you can do so that your client feels that he or she got more than what was expected?

_____

_____

_____

_____

_____

"This is mind-blowing. This makes total sense, Dan. I didn't realize what it takes to be a salon owner. All the things you've just shared with me – raising my prices, attracting the right clients, creating the right experience – they go way beyond knowing how to cut great hair," Simone starts to realize.

THERE ARE MORE REASONS TO GO HIGHER

For those who have been reading up to this page and are still not convinced it's time to increase your prices, let me show you the list of benefits you are missing.

Benefit #1: With higher prices, you have higher profit margins to pay better, more productive, loyal employees.

Benefit #2: With higher prices, you will have more profits to invest in better equipment and high-quality products. It also gives you and your staff the ability to spend more time building solid relationships with your clients.

Benefit #3: (The BEST REASON in my opinion!) Having high prices raises your clients' expectations of your salon.

When someone goes to a low-price salon, they expect problems. They know corners may be cut, so the question in their mind as they enter that salon is, *"What are they going to do wrong?"* You know that when people expect a problem, no matter how good your work is, they will uncover something to prove they are right. That is simply how our minds work.

When someone goes to a high-end salon, they expect the best. They know they've picked the best salon, and expect to be pleased by the experience.

By changing the psychology of the experience through your price and the relationship-building steps you've put in place before your client comes to your salon, your client is expecting to be happy instead of unhappy.

This is why having higher prices is, in itself, a marketing strategy.

By raising your prices, you will be worth more to your clients.

Clients know that they get what they pay for.

Take an example of two best friends who go shopping separately to buy the same Louis Vuitton handbag. They come back from shopping and go to Starbucks to compare their new goodies. One said she paid only $400 for the handbag. The other said she paid way more – $2,000. Right away, we can tell that the cheaper handbag is likely a fake, the more expensive handbag is the authentic one. The girls probably compared the stitching, the zipper, the serial number stamped in the bags to confirm which is fake, which is real. And the cheaper one is deemed less desirable. The more expensive one is deemed more desirable.

It's a never-ending positive cycle!

The more people pay, the more they appreciate what they have.

When your clients pay you top price, they will help you make sure it has been a valuable experience. They will help you justify the price.

Isn't that amazing?

I know for a fact if you were to pay $1,000 for this book, you would have paid more attention, taken more notes, and would be more likely and willing to apply the strategies I am teaching you.

The more you charge your clients, create an experience with lots of value, the more your clients' behaviors will improve for the better. Soon, they'll be referring their friends and neighbors, because they want to feel good about their decision to buy your services. Now they have a stake in making their buying experience valuable, and they will help you make your value a reality.

If you think your low price is showing respect for your client. It's not.

It's showing a lack of respect for your client and for yourself. If you appreciate yourself enough to raise your prices and say, "I'm worth it," then people will know you are worth it. People will value you to the degree that you value yourself.

The higher price itself attracts the right type of clients with the right attitude, which makes the entire experience better for both you and them.

Lokism #45

"Just by raising your prices you will be worth more to your clients."

LOW IS NOT THE WAY TO GO

"Now, Simone, I hope you understand all the reasons why lowering your prices is not the way to run your business," I affirm.

"Yes," she sighs with a heavy heart. "Lowering my prices was actually helping me put my salon out of business!"

It is a big A-HA moment for Simone.

I emphasize, "By lowering your prices, you took home less on every single transaction. There was less to go around, less for your stylists, less for yourself. Less for your stylists to continue training at the higher level, less for you to pay good employees."

"And Simone… another problem with low price-positioning is that salons get stuck in that cheap format. It becomes a part of their identity and it deepens their fear of ever being more expensive than someone else. With time, they slowly start to believe the only reason a client is choosing them is because they're a little less expensive!"

I continue, "Did you know? There's yet another damaging impact to your salon that low prices cause."

"There's more?" Simone can't believe the long list of "no-nos."

I say, "It's subtler, but as toxic: Low prices attract more questionable clients. The price shoppers are not the kinds of clients you want in the long run, anyway!

"To build a business that serves you, instead of a business that you're constantly serving, you want to keep improving the quality of your clients. You want loyal, long-term clients. You want people who can afford your services over and over again. You want people who refer others like them," I say.

"Low prices attract disloyal, unfaithful clients. Clients you can't build a business on. These price shoppers, they take up all your time.

You can spend hours and hours trying to sell to somebody and all they do is negotiate and negotiate," I conclude.

I dislike price shoppers with a passion. And I am going to make sure Simone understands why. "They also do all the complaining. They're whiners. Troublemakers. But they are keen to brag about how little they paid you. Loyalty is their only price. They may only buy from you once [which is the most expensive cost of acquiring a client], then they are going elsewhere to find a lower price than yours."

"I completely understand it now," Simone notes.

She confesses, "I'm glad I was part of this group-coaching session today. I'll admit, it was a little nerve-wrecking at first. But now, I see what my mistakes were. Those discounts I was blindly giving away thinking it would make me more competitive – were actually de-valuing my salon. It was doing the complete opposite. No more low-balling my prices! I need to increase my salon prices so clients think more highly of my salon, of my stylists, and they will value their experience even more. And I get to take home more money!

"Dan, you've given me a lot of insights on running a successful salon. I've got to rethink my business strategy, how to attract the right clients, how to put in place a pull-marketing system to have clients lining up for my services. More importantly, I need to decide how to create the right experience for them."

I am elated hearing that Simone was making this mental shift. It's a big step for her.

"Simone, you're clearly passionate about keeping your business alive. That's awesome! It's going to be a whole new beginning for you, now that you have the knowledge on how to run a profitable salon. I have EVERY confidence you can turn things around for Chester Hair Salon."

About seven months later, Simone stood up and shared with us her amazing transformation... "Hey everyone!" exclaimed Simone. "I've gotten off the sinking ship!"

She couldn't contain her excitement. The whole group could feel it . "I used the strategies you taught me at our last group meeting. At first, I was a little apprehensive about how things would turn out – I was doing things totally different from before. You know, raising prices... and then, business started picking up. It was unbelievable... now my chairs are full every weekend. We are booked at least a week ahead!"

"That's incredible to hear how you've turned things around!" I was thrilled for her.

"Dan, with more money coming in now, I've even upgraded some of my equipment in the salon. My stylists are happy, clients are happy... Chester Hair Salon even got nominated in the local papers for the No. 1 local hair salon. Our books look good, we are making a profit again. No more seeing red!" Simone declared.

She continued, "Things are really looking promising for me. I can't thank you enough. I couldn't have done this without you. To show you a token of my sincerest appreciation, I've bought you a gift. I know how much you love books, it's a Kindle. Thank you so very much."

"And I want to thank you guys. You are an amazing group of people and I am honored to be able to be a part of this group. Thank you so much for helping me, supporting me, and believing in me!

I LOVE YOU ALL SO MUCH!!!"

I got choked up... Everyone got up and gave Simone a hug. It was absolutely wonderful.

LIE #7

"I COULD DO THIS ON MY OWN"

*"I absolutely believe that people, unless coached,
never reach their maximum capabilities".*

– Bob Nardelli, former CEO, Home Depot and Chrysler

LIE #7

This is a story about a young boy.

He immigrated to North America when he was 13 years old. And even though he couldn't speak or write a word of English, his parents put him in public school – like everyone else.

Because of his limited English, he had a difficult time communicating with other people. As a result, he didn't speak much to anyone. And he didn't really have any friends.

Other students thought he was a weirdo. They weren't very kind to him, constantly made fun of him. Some bullies even beat him up on several occasions.

Life was hard on the young boy.

He would always sit in the back of the classroom all by himself.

Most of the time, he had no idea what the teacher was saying. Still, he would never put up his hand to ask questions because he was afraid of being embarrassed because of the way he spoke.

He didn't want to be a laughingstock to his classmates, so he pretty much suffered in silence.

And every day after school, the young boy would race back home and lock himself in his room and watch TV – alone.

Can you blame him?

Can you imagine going to a foreign country where you couldn't speak or write the language? How could you possibly make friends or expect to do well in school?

The learning curve was simply too steep, too sharp.

As time went on, the young boy became more and more depressed. He completely lost his self-esteem. In fact, the young boy felt so sorry for himself he would walk around with his head hung down. When he did speak with anyone, he avoided looking at them straight in the eyes.

Because of his limited English knowledge, the young boy barely passed any of his subjects at school.

One day, he actually flunked one of the exams – geography. His teacher was disgusted with him and said, "Do you know that you got the lowest score on this exam? I've never had a student that is as stupid as you."

But the teacher didn't stop there!

He also said, "If you don't pull your socks up, you'll never graduate from high school."

The young boy didn't know what to say…what could he say?

He just stood there and started to cry.

That just made things worse.

The teacher looked at the young boy (who was wiping the tears that were running down his cheeks), and uttered the most demoralizing thing the boy had ever heard, "You're hopeless! Nothing but a crybaby! You'll never amount to anything in your life. Get out of my office!"

That crushed the young boy's heart.

It delivered such a blow to the young boy – emotionally and mentally – that he went home, locked himself in his room and cried his eyes out.

He thought to himself, "I hate school. I hate my parents. I hate my instructors. I hate everyone. Maybe that teacher is right. I am stupid. I am a loser."

As if that humiliation wasn't enough, a couple of days later, the most terrifying thing imaginable happened to the young boy. He found out he had to do a mandatory three-minute oral presentation in front of his whole English class.

He was absolutely terrified. He couldn't sleep…he couldn't eat…he couldn't think about anything except how scared he was.

Finally, even though he was scared and embarrassed, he approached his English teacher and said, "Miss Fallon, I don't want to do my presentation. I am too afraid."

Fortunately, Miss Fallon knew a lot about children and about teaching in way that connects with young boys.

Instead of yelling at him, she just asked him, "What seems to be the problem?"

The young boy said shakingly, "I just can't do it. I just can't do it. I just can't do it. People will laugh at me."

She didn't make fun of his fears. She listened to the young boy as he confided in her all of his worries, all of his concerns.

After listening, she told him, "Nobody's going to laugh at you. If they do, I'll punish them. Remember, in order to graduate from this class, you have to do the presentation. It's one of the requirements."

Miss Fallon then said, "I know exactly how to help you. There's still a week's time before the presentation. Why don't you come to my office after school? You can practice and I'll be your audience. OK?

The young boy thought about it for a moment and finally said, "OK." And for the first time in a long time, he thought that things might actually be all right.

Finally the Big Day arrived.

He was nervous, but he had been practicing with Miss Fallon for a whole week.

Still, his heart was racing like the wind. His palms were sweaty. He felt like he was going to

Lokism #46

" Never underestimate the power of someone believing in you."

throw up or pass out. Then it dawned on him that he understood what others meant by, "I'd rather die than do public speaking."

The young boy doubted himself, but he had something else going for him.

A promise that he'd made to himself – that he won't "chicken out" and disappoint Miss Fallon, after all she had done for him. He couldn't let her down.

And he didn't!

His three-minute presentation went smoothly from start to finish.

When it was all over, the young boy said to himself, "They didn't laugh at me. They didn't make fun of me. People actually applauded... WOW!"

It was only a three-minute speech, but for the little boy, it was a turning point in his life.

It was a declaration of independence. It gave him self-esteem and shot his confidence through the roof!

This transformation was made possible because of Miss Fallon. She worked with the young boy, mentored him from a "nobody" to a successful "somebody".

She completely changed his life in the most positive way possible!

Slowly, the young boy began to have a better understanding of the English language. As his English improved, his grades also improved. He successfully graduated from high school and went to college.

As a young man, he joined Toastmasters International so he could conquer his fear of public speaking. With his new confidence and drive, the young man completed the Competent Toastmaster course in just 2½ months; most people typically spend from 6 to 10 months completing the course.

To no one's surprise, the young man was elected president of his Toastmaster Club. He became the youngest person in his province to hold the office. Under his leadership, the club received the prestigious "President Distinguished" award from Toastmasters International that year.

The young boy who once spoke no English and was considered the least likely to succeed is now a multimillionaire and successful entrepreneur running many profitable businesses.

He has achieved total financial freedom. He's now a highly respected expert in his industry.

The young boy who once almost threw up because of his fear of public speaking is now a best-selling author who speaks to tens of thousands of people yearly. His presence truly captivates his audience from his opening words till the close.

Never in his wildest dreams would the young boy have ever imagined he would one day actually speak and write for a living.

Today, he spends his time giving back to others, mentoring and coaching them to discover their personal greatness – the same way he found his.

> **Lokism #47**
>
> "The salon business is a team sport."

With the culture shock, language barrier, and the obstacles a young boy faces, his road to success as an adult would NOT have been possible IF he had to do it on his own.

Miss Fallon made it happen for him – and with him.

She took him under her wing, and, with her patience and tutelage, recognized the young boy's talents and unleashed the greatness buried within him, thereby transforming him from a nobody to a somebody.

The story of this young boy is completely 100% true because it's the story of my life – Dan Lok.

THE UNVARNISHED TRUTH ABOUT WHAT IT REALLY TAKES TO SUCCEED

The best salon owners are great leaders. And great leaders know how to build great teams. Salon owners who always work in their business not only do not see the forest for the trees, but usually they try to do everything themselves. Salon owners who work on their business maintain a birds-eye view of the business and the world around it.

You may think you know the answer to this simple question: "Who actually invented the light bulb?" The 1st light bulb was built by Humphry Davy (an Englishman) in 1809. Thomas Alva Edison improved the invention and based his improvements on a patent he purchased from inventors Henry Woodward & Matthew Evans who patented their bulb in 1875.

We like to think of Thomas Alva Edison sitting in isolation, working alone, day after day, flicking the switch on one failed light bulb experiment after another.

Maybe he was even motivating himself in the dark with the now-famous words, "I have not failed. I've just found ten thousand ways that won't work."

That's the myth. Here's the Edison reality.

Good old Thomas Alva had a packed lab – a pool of 21 assistants and support staff!

A shocker, isn't it?

When asked one day why he employed a team of 21 assistants, Edison replied, "If I could solve all the problems myself, I would."

He knew that teams are the critical factor in business success. Edison isn't the only one who discovered that.

A more contemporary example is basketball great Michael Jordan.

When asked to describe the importance of teams in playing sports, he said, "Talent wins games, but teamwork wins championships."

Even the superstar athlete recognizes one can't reach the pinnacle alone.

Anyone who has succeeded in any endeavor has done so through a great team. Wealthy salon owners know enough to understand that they do not need to do everything themselves. There's just not enough time in the day or energy in their bodies.

FOUR EXIT STRATEGIES FOR YOUR SALON BUSINESS

Let me ask you a question: Where do you see yourself and your business five years from now?

This is very important, because if you don't know where you're going, you'll probably end up somewhere else.

When you follow the advice I've laid out in this book, you'll have four appealing choices for your future, as well as your business:

Scenario #1 – You can keep your business, continue to work hands-on, remain active in the daily salon operations, and strive to make a huge income.

Scenario #2 – You can keep your business, delegate the day-to-day operations, come in to your business, say, once a week, and make a steady monthly income.

Scenario #3 – You can expand your business with multiple locations and maybe turn into a franchise operation.

Scenario #4 – You can sell your business for a substantial lump sum and retire early.

In order to achieve this "hands-off" approach and still receive a steady income from your salon business, you need to start building a great team.

Remember, good old Thomas Alva had a packed lab of 21 assistants and support staff. Running your business alone doesn't make you wealthy; building a team and delegating responsibilities to them does.

By having a staff-driven salon, the staff fuels your salon growth and eventually takes the pressure off you and puts the fun and joy back in being a true salon owner.

I BECAME A BETTER LEADER WHEN I LEARNED THIS

When I embarked on the road to transform myself from wimpy kid to student extraordinaire, I had Miss Fallon on my team.

Likewise, salon owners need to choose their staff wisely.

Let me ask you: What kind of employee do you want?

You will probably answer: punctual, gets the job done, experienced, talented, positive attitude, and loyal.

Yes, those are some very good qualities to look out for.

But the only kind of employee I want is a profitable employee. Period!

What's the point of having an extra person in your salon if that person does not generate you more revenue than the cost of actually having that person in your salon? The only reason to have an employee is profit.

Don't fool yourself thinking it's your responsibility to provide your staff with a job, so they can pay their bills and take care of their family.

Or think that you need to make every employee in your salon happy in order for them to be productive. Don't get me wrong. That doesn't mean that you should be insensitive to employees' working conditions, health benefits, fringe benefits, and compensation. In fact, my rule on that is give as much as you can.

However, a happy workplace doesn't equal a productive workplace. Our employees are happiest not when we focus on them, but when we lead them to focus on our services and our clients.

The role of the salon owner is to provide employees with a positive work environment. Your employees need to be productive, finding satisfaction in delivering great value and service.

If your salon business goes under, your employees may not even feel sorry for you, they would just go look for another job. Your employees are responsible for keeping their own jobs.

They need to make themselves indispensable for you.

Not the other way around.

"Coming together is a beginning. Keeping together is progress. Working together is success."

– Henry Ford

SET A HIGH STANDARD FOR YOUR SALON

In the salon business, you are managing people for profit.

I've known of other salon owners who have had to put up with totally unacceptable employee behavior such as:

- Eating in the front desk

- Refusing to do repetitive tasks

- Coming in to work late

- Dressing inappropriately for work

- Treating clients with disrespect

Anytime this happens, you need to step up and take care of the problem ASAP.

Don't let the little things slide.

Little things, if shrugged off, invite anarchy. It sends the message to the troublemaker that you can be bossed around, that he or she can challenge you. Even though you are the boss, you're just a nominal figurehead.

Trouble in your salon is like a virus. Something small that goes undetected will start to spread like wildfire – soon crippling every single facet of your business.

When an employee – any employee – becomes a detriment to your salon for any reason, that employee is just like a cracked window. The ripple effect from his or her failure, however slight, can completely shatter your business.

Slowly but surely, you will lose respect as a salon owner. You will lose control over your employees. And you will lose control over your salon – period.

Don't try to be a "nice boss" so you can be liked by all your employees. This is not a popularity contest. You need to be an effective boss.

You need to uphold a high standard for your salon, and ensure your employees are living up to your expectations.

Set the bar high – it's the only way to be successful.

ESTABLISH A WORKING SYSTEM FOR YOUR SALON

Have you heard of Murphy's Law? It states, "Anything that can go wrong, will go wrong." Believe me, Murphy will knock on your door and pay a visit to your salon or spa.

Lokism #49

"If you don't alter the salon environment, there's no implementation."

Human error, computer glitches, and miscommunications will inevitably disrupt your system at some point. Having a plan in place to solve problems will make the difference between keeping and losing a client!

Begin by outlining duties for each and every staff member, and work your way up the accountability ladder.

Pay attention to detail. Plan for every possible scenario that could affect your clients and develop solutions for each one of these challenges.

Develop specific procedures for every job in your salon, so that your business will run smoothly, almost automatically, like a well-oiled machine.

Assume nothing and include everything.

What must employees do to make things go right? What must employees do when things go wrong? What must they do if the procedure doesn't work?

What if that doesn't work, either? All these questions must be answered.

GETTING YOUR STAFF TO SUPPORT THE NEW SYSTEM

All that time you spent creating your salon systems is useless unless you get your employees to implement them and implement them consistently.

That's the only way to guarantee the salon quality you desire.

You're not just the boss. You're the leader, the educator, the coach, the trainer, and sometimes even the cheerleader.

Everyone is resistant to change; it's human nature. I understand.

People don't like to be forced out of their comfort zones and often resent new policies and procedures introduced into the business, especially if they've worked somewhere for a long time.

You will hear, "I already know how to do that," or "I like the old way better," or "I don't think the new procedure will work."

So how do you solve this problem? It's simple.

You must let them know what's in it for them.

It's your responsibility as a salon owner to determine what is best for your business, share your vision with your employees, and sell them on the benefits.

Explain to your employees why you are making changes and the importance of the system for the continued success of your salon business. Explain the importance of a business system, and how, once implemented, this system will make their jobs easier because it will take the guesswork out of resolving difficult situations.

"Leadership is the art of getting someone else to do something you want done because he wants to do it."
– Dwight Eisenhower

When introducing systems, I also find it very beneficial to attach some sort of an incentive.

It helps smooth out any "operational bumps" your staff will encounter with the changes.

Remember, your frontline employees are the ones who are talking and interacting with your clients. An incentive program will go a long way.

After a few months, you may want to switch to a team incentive so employees begin working together and applying the new procedures for a group reward.

By the way, public recognition is also a fantastic way to reinforce progress for learning the system. Change can always be positive. You just need to be creative and make the experience fun and exciting, too.

Now that we've discussed the importance of teams to help you work in your business, let's focus on how you can work on your business.

THE MOST IMPORTANT PERSON TO MAKE ALL YOUR DREAMS A REALITY

If your little daughter wants to learn ballet, you'll find her a dance class with a ballet teacher. If your son wants to play soccer, you'll find a soccer team with a great coach. If one of your children struggles with math, you'll find a math tutor.

In other words, you find suitable opportunities for your children to be properly mentored in sports, in Scouts or Brownies, in music or dance, and in their education.

Did it ever occur that you also need the same mentoring for your salon business?

Mentoring isn't just for the young people. Everyone, regardless of age, gender, education, background, can benefit from mentoring.

"It's not hard work and experience that make for success, it's doing what works."

Unfortunately, most adults do not seek such help for themselves. They believe they need to do it on their own.

With your salon business, I can bet that you're fiercely independent.

You have an "I can do it on my own" attitude. You're tired of letting someone else call the shots when you can do a better job yourself, especially if you've worked for other salons,

Well, this renegade "do-it-yourself" mind-set can be one of your greatest strengths as a salon owner. When you are forced to be 100% accountable for your results (or lack thereof), you become highly motivated to create your own success.

However, having a lone wolf mind-set can create a whole lot of problems, too.

When you hit a roadblock, you don't have anyone to turn to for guidance.

Answers that would be a phone call away can often turn into lengthy days of frustration and a lot of wasted money and time when you're doing it all by yourself.

And worse, you may never solve the problem – running into dead end after dead end. So your problems persist. And you continue struggling in your salon business. One of the biggest lies salon owners believe is you can do this on your own.

On your own, you do only what makes sense to you.

With a mentor, you are provided with ideas and thoughts that at first may seem somewhat contradictory, but might actually be much better.

If your salon business is struggling, you can't keep doing the same things over and over again and expect different results.

"Insanity is defined as doing the same thing over and over again and expecting different results."
– Albert Einstein

To make a giant leap forward in your life, you need to do what does NOT make sense to you.

Only a very wise mentor can alert you to such new and strange actions you could take to make a huge change in your life.

You went to school or college and invested hundreds of hours to master your craft.

Why won't you invest that in your salon BUSINESS? Get the mentoring you need for your business.

And see for yourself what a mentored life could really be.

HOW I FOUND MY MENTORS (AND HOW YOU CAN, TOO)

You already know, one of my main mentors was Miss Fallon when I was in high school.

Lokism #51

" Most people are drowning in information, yet they are starving for wisdom."

But what you may not know is that even though I am highly successful today, I am continually working with mentors, 30 or 40 nowadays.

I made one-on-one contact with some of them. Others, I've never actually met. They wouldn't know me if I walked past them on the street.

But I've experienced their guidance through books, CDs, DVDs, home-study courses, online coaching programs, and seminars.

During my business career, I always seek guidance from mentors – experienced businesspeople who are already successful.

I realize good information is hard to come by in the real world, and access to a mentor who can give you the inside scoop on what's working, and what's not working, is invaluable.

From what books to read to how to create and write a promotion to what software to use, I rely on my mentors.

And I'm not embarrassed to admit that I pay just ONE of my mentors $100,000 a year, because I make that investment back 10 times over!

Now, I can already hear some of you saying, "Dan, if you're already very successful, what do you need mentors for?"

I have mentors for the same reason that Dr. Phil McGraw has Oprah Winfrey as his mentor. Dr. Phil rose to fame after appearing several times on The Oprah Winfrey Show. He eventually launched his own TV program, Dr. Phil. In an interview, he attributed his success to Oprah Winfrey, as she was the person who taught him everything he knows about television.

"For every one of us that succeeds, it's because there's somebody there to show you the way out."
– Oprah Winfrey

My mentors give me a fresh perspective on my marketing angles, open my eyes to exciting new ideas and revenue streams, and use their experience to help me avoid costly mistakes.

If I have a reason I can't do something, they show me how I can! They don't let me make excuses. They give me access to new resources and contacts, many times their own personal contacts.

My mentors guide me down the direct path of success. I am a big believer that there's no need to reinvent the wheel or go through the school of hard knocks. Mentors point out roadblocks and potential dangers in your business. They show you mistakes that could happen, so you can take steps to avoid the mistakes.

It's extremely powerful to have someone watching over you like this, helping you avoid pitfalls and common mistakes, holding your hand each step of the way as you walk down the path of success.

Over the years, my mentors have helped me save and generate millions of dollars.

That's why I firmly believe that – whether you're just getting started or you're already extremely successful – you can always be more successful with a mentor.

THE SHORTCUT TO CREATING THE SALON BUSINESS YOU'VE ALWAYS IMAGINED (BUT STILL HAVE A LIFE)

Think back to when you were in school. There were probably many teachers, but I'm quite sure there was one who was your favorite. Someone like my Miss Fallon, who took the time to give you the attention and help you needed.

Imagine if all your teachers were as wonderful as that one teacher. What a different life you'd have.

Now, think of your salon business, and let me show you a few benefits of working with a mentor.

1. Supercharge Your Marketing

End hit-or-miss, unsuccessful, wasteful advertising. Your mentor can teach you truly proven, effective methods of attracting a steady stream of good, respectful, quality-oriented clients.

Your mentor can guide you to implement marketing systems that make your cash flow and your business stronger, healthier, and much more predictable.

2. Get More Done in Less Time

When you work alone, your lack of experience and perspective can cause you to waste time on certain areas of your salon business.

Think about it: greeting clients, answering the phones, booking and confirming appointments, responding to emails, keeping the salon clean, dealing with no-show employees, ordering supplies, creating a marketing promotions calendar, payroll, banking, etc.

Your mentor can help you identify repetitive, time-consuming tasks.

Your mentor will also show you quick, easy, and inexpensive ways to outsource or even automate these tasks so that you're working ON your business, not IN your business!

3. Get honest, informed advice

To me, a mentor is someone who cares deeply about your success. This person should be someone you admire, trust and feel comfortable sharing your triumphs and your struggles with.

Someone who'll give it to you straight is one of the most valuable assets you can have in business.

Your mentor can also act as a sounding board for your ideas and plans. You can bounce concepts off your mentor and expect honest, no-sugar-coated feedback.

Lokism #52

"You are only as good as your support group."

4. Develop accountability and motivation

A good mentor will hold you accountable and will ask more of you than you will ask of yourself. Your mentor will provide support as you broaden your scope of responsibilities.

A lot of salon owners struggle with implementing ideas. Sometimes, it's hard enough trying to keep up with the day-to-day challenges and a million other things. Even if you want to work on your business, sometimes you just don't have the time and you don't have the energy or desire.

Your mentor can inspire you to build your business by reigniting the passion that got you so fired up when you first opened your salon. Remember the excitement, pride, and maybe fear when you opened your salon?

Your mentor is your best friend – even when you can be your own worst enemy.

5. Skip the learning curve – and avoid costly mistakes

With the guidance of an experienced mentor, you can skip the learning curve and do what's already been proven to work, right out of the starting gate.

You can avoid the costly mistakes and fast-track your success so you see profits sooner.

6. Make more money

It's been my experience that salon owners who work with personal mentors are way more successful than salon owners who don't.

This is because your mentor's only job is to make you more confident, more effective, and ultimately more profitable than your competitors.

When you succeed, so do they.

HOW DO YOU FIND THE RIGHT MENTOR FOR YOU?

Now that you know how a mentor can help you grow your salon business, you're probably wondering how you can find one.

This can actually be a very difficult step.

Traditionally, a mentor would be a successful entrepreneur who recognized some special qualities in you and took you under his or her wing.

However, you're probably working in your salon most of the time, and the people you see the most often are your kids, your spouse, your staff or your clients!

Hundreds of people are now marketing themselves as "salon gurus" or "beauty business consultants." They recognize that there is money to be made selling their services to eager professionals like you.

The bad news is that most of them won't help you make a dime.

Why? Most of the people positioning themselves as gurus or consultants are people who have failed – often repeatedly – in their own salon business ventures.

Or worse, they have never owned a salon.

They figure it is easier to teach success than actually achieve it themselves.

Tell me: would you hire a personal trainer who is 30 to 50 pounds overweight?

Don't get me wrong. I believe everyone has a right to make a living.

But I have serious problems with people passing themselves off as something they're not.

Lokism #53

"Become an expert at finding experts."

As one of my mentors told me many years ago, "Dan, if you want to be a millionaire, you better learn from one."

Always, always, always consider the source.

So before you choose a mentor, check his or her credentials.

Mentor with someone who has achieved the results you want in your salon business. Then follow that person's path of success and make it your own.

If the mentor has courses or material he or she has specialized in, spend some time investigating it. Learn about the person's background and training. After all, this is a person you'll be entrusting your future success to.

You are going to be working with your mentor for months or even years.

It's a long-term business relationship, and you want it to be as pleasant as it is productive.

Having mentors in my business turned out great for me.

It works for my students.

It works for champion athletes.

It works for millionaire entrepreneurs, and I know it will work for you.

Get a mentor today and watch your business and your life transform in ways you've never thought possible.

CONCLUSION

Well, if you've made it all the way here, I want to congratulate you.

I know that's a lot of information to digest. Most salon owners get into this business believing the seven lies I've identified in previous chapters. And believing them is stifling the growth of their salon business.

I've done my best to explain why they are nothing but lies by sharing with you my personal transformation from poor grocery boy to successful salon owner.

But I am more than that.

I'm also a mentor.

Don't confuse me with a "beauty business consultant." There's a huge difference.

The market is saturated with every Tom, Dick or Harry passing themselves off as a guru because they know there is money to be made from struggling salon owners desperate for help. Some of them may have been salon owners years ago, or are just teaching what they've studied, but actually haven't "been there, done that." They are not necessarily active in the beauty industry, per se.

Mentors like myself actively do what they teach. In other words, I eat my own cooking. No lip service. I come from the school of hard knocks, where my life experience, struggle, failures, flaws, and rise to success came from using various techniques, strategies and systems. I understand what you are going through and how you operate in your day-to-day business life. You can immediately use my knowledge to solve immediate problems, and even use them to help you tackle future challenges in your salon.

I HAVE "been there, done that," I know exactly what it takes to run a successful salon business. My salon has been turning in a profit since our second month in business. We make a solid six-figure income a year from it. I'm a real-life, successful salon-business owner who still owns and operates a salon. And I'm only at my salon a few hours per week.

I've been teaching real-world strategies and salon-business fundamentals to many salon and spa owners around the world. Whether you're a new salon, or a salon needing a complete makeover, I can take your business to the next level.

I know that the information I've written in this book is contradictory to the mainstream, and, as a result, can be overwhelming.

But understand that this is a new way of doing business, a new way of thinking, a new way of living.

People are resistant to change because of the fear of the unknown. That's normal.

The good news is that I've shown you the strategies and systems I've used to run a flourishing salon business. You now have a blueprint of what you need to do. But the blueprint is only as good as you make it.

You need to get focused and take serious action.

To assist you in your next phase, I've put together a short, seven-step action plan for you:

STEP # 1 – TEACH AND SHARE WHAT YOU'VE LEARNED FROM THIS BOOK TO OTHERS IMMEDIATELY.

Teach the strategies to your staff, your manager, or your business partner. You will find your understanding deepens when you have to teach someone else.

Over the years, I've learned that the best way to really learn something is to teach the concept or strategy to someone else. Anytime you have to teach something, you are forced to plan, think and act on what you have learned, which really drives it home.

STEP # 2 – SET ASIDE TWO TO THREE HOURS PER WEEK TO SIMPLY THINK ABOUT YOUR BUSINESS.

You might say, "Dan, I think about my business all the time, it's all I do while driving down the street, even when I'm eating lunch or taking a shower."

Well, that's not exactly what I have in mind. Worrying is NOT thinking.

Think about the bottlenecks and constraints in your business and ways to eliminate them This is essential to YOUR FREEDOM.

Think about how you can work more ON your business, rather than IN your business.

Setting some time aside for reflection will clarify and amplify the context and meaning behind the experiences you are having that day, week, month or year in your business.

Learning happens best when you give yourself time to be alone so that what is learned may be internalized and used again.

If you don't have time to sit alone and think, to research, to study ways to improve your business, then I strongly suggest you get help to work ON your business by having a mentor. In the previous chapter, I mentioned the importance of mentoring with someone who has achieved the results you want in your salon business, and to follow his or her path of success.

STEP # 3 – IMPLEMENT A SYSTEM THAT WILL ATTRACT QUALITY CLIENTS SO YOU CAN CHARGE ABOVE-AVERAGE PRICES AND PROFIT MORE FROM EACH VISIT.

My salon business depends heavily on this ONE method of marketing, with 60 percent of all my new clients coming from: the Internet.

The Internet is the most effective and productive means I know for getting your phones ringing and filling up your appointment book.

If you don't have a website, set one up immediately. You can't afford not to. If you already have a website, make sure it's optimized for search engines so your potential clients can find you. Get your business listed on Google. Keep tweaking and testing until you are on the first page. Set up a Facebook page and update it regularly.

If you need help, I've put together a team of people that that will actually do all of the above for you to help you attract more clients and create the business you really want.

It's an automated done-for-you marketing service with the kind of power that could save yourself hours and hours of precious time while you devote your time to other important areas of your business (And spend more time with your loved ones!)

However, due to the incredible support we provide to our clients, we can only take on a few new clients per month. We operate on a first-come-first-served basis.

If you want to put your name on the waiting list, contact my office at: www.SalonBusinessExpert.com.

STEP # 4 – IMPLEMENT A SYSTEM THAT WILL AUTOMATICALLY GET YOUR CLIENTS TO COME BACK TO YOU MORE OFTEN.

Reward your loyal clients by giving them an exceptional experience. Go the extra mile and show them they you care. Show that you value their business and support.

Do this by capturing every client's contact information. This way, you can keep in touch with them. It could be to welcome them to the program or remember their birthday, anniversary or other special occasion. It also gives you reason to contact them on weekly specials and upcoming salon promotions.

Using a good software, I'm in contact with all my clients, but I never have to create a client database. I never have to design and test marketing pieces, take them to the printer, address and stamp the postcards. I never have to hire extra staff to manage the additional workload.

With a good software, all of this happens on autopilot. It's literally freed me up to work on my business, instead of in it.

You can take a look at the system I am using, or you can develop your own. Whatever you do, capture client data and follow up with them in a timely manner, and before you know it, you'll see your salon prosper.

STEP # 5 – MAXIMIZE CLIENT VALUE.

Once you have a system for attracting clients, a system for bringing back existing clients, and keeping clients longer, your next step is to upsell your clients on your products and other services.

Teach your staff the art of upselling. It could range from a simple recommendation of retail products that will benefit the client to bundled services at a higher dollar amount to offering prepaid packages (focusing on the savings percentage).

You want to set up membership programs to lock-in renewing and continuing stable income from your A-List clients.

As demand exceeds supply, you can raise your prices and keep increasing the value of what you offer.

STEP # 6 – HIRE GREAT PEOPLE SO YOU CAN WORK LESS.

After you've established these marketing systems, your income will skyrocket, and you'll have a steady flow of new, high-quality clients. Your appointment books will be filled up all the time. Your clients will cheerfully pay you higher and premium prices because they value your exceptional services.

You can stop trading hours for dollars.

You now have the ability and money to hire better staff and put a manager in place.

Your employees are motivated to stay with you because they are generously rewarded for their efforts.

You have created a great working environment that even attracts your competitor's employees who want to come work for you!

It's easier for you to attract and retain good people because you've create a positive, productive work environment.

You have less stress.

You cut back your working hours and you work with clients only if you want to.

STEP # 7 - ENJOY THE BENEFITS!

You now finally have the clients, the money, and the freedom that you envisioned when you started your salon.

Life is an adventure! Life is a journey! Life is exciting! Life's opportunities are infinite. Go on that vacation. Buy that dream car. Buy that dream home.

Please send me your success story. I get an adrenaline rush just hearing about the progress made by my readers and students around the world.

Tell me all about your accomplishments and progress. I want to know all about them.

I would love to meet you in person at our live training events, where I could work with you more closely and take your salon business to the next level.

For resources that support the principles in this book, I invite you to go to www.SalonBusinessExpert.com. This site will feature and regularly update all of the resources and tools that will help you grow your salon business.

And "LIKE" my facebook page to connect with other owners around the world: www.facebook.com/salonbusinessexpert.

BOOK DAN LOK AND MAKE YOUR EVENT UNFORGETTABLE!

Would you like Dan Lok to speak to your audience? Excellent! You are making the right decision. Here's why: Dan is known for consistently receiving the highest overall speaker rating at major conferences.

As an author, master trainer and brilliant communicator who is also a successful entrepreneur owning and operating multiple businesses including a highly successful salon, Dan brings enthusiasm, insight, and energy to his presentations. In the years that he has been a speaker and a coach, he has delivered powerful messages to thousands of business owners and entrepreneurs.

Dan's high-impact, dynamic entertaining style moves people to action. He travels the world teaching salon and spa owners – whether one-on-on or to audiences of 1,000 or more – how to experience unparalleled revenue and personal growth, financial freedom and overall happiness.

Dan and his team understand the challenges and pressures of event planners and his focus is to make, you the event planner, shine like the hero you truly are. Event attendees, your event team and management will all be congratulating you on what a great job you have done by inviting Dan Lok to speak at your event.

"Dan delivers a dynamic, actionable business blueprint that can turn any salon/spa business, in any city, in any economy into a powerhouse."

Dan has the unique ability to emotionally connect and mentally engage salon or spa owners from all walks of life because he's "been there and done that" as a salon owner himself. He draws upon his personal experience, business wisdom, and cutting-edge trends to deliver a powerful, content-rich presentation.

The bottom line is Dan promises and he delivers. What matters most is your agenda and your desired results. He believes that presentations have no power unless they relate with your audience members and connect with them at a core level not just at the event, but long after. With a rigorous pre-event preparation process, Dan and his team will ensure your investment and his talk are crafted to best meet your specific event and audience needs and outcomes.

To continue to maintain an optimal quality of life and to pursue his diverse business interests, Dan is increasingly selective about the speaking engagements he will now accept.

For inquiries into booking Dan for your next event, please contact us at speaking@salonbusinessexpert.com.